The Bush Is Burning!

Radical Judaism Faces the
Pharaohs of the Modern Superstate

Arthur I. Waskow

The Macmillan Company, New York, New York

The Macmillan Company
866 Third Avenue, New York, N.Y. 10022
Collier-Macmillan Canada Ltd., Toronto, Ontario

Library of Congress Catalog Card Number: 79-163231

First Macmillan Paperbacks Edition 1971

Printed in the United States of America

The Bush Is Burning!

Other Books by Arthur I. Waskow

The Limits of Defense (with Marcus G. Raskin)
America in Hiding (with Stanley L. Newman)
The Worried Man's Guide to World Peace
From Race Riot to Sit-in, 1919 and the 1960s
The Debate over Thermonuclear Strategy (editor)
The Freedom Seder: A New Haggadah for Passover
Running Riot

For my sisters and brothers
of Jews for Urban Justice
in Washington, D.C. (the diaspora of the
Diaspora) and of the radical Jewish movement across
America—who agree with some of this and disagree
with some of it, but who taught me all of it.

Chesed umishpat ashira,
L'chau Adonai azamira!

לדוד מזמור
חסד־ומשפט אשירה
לך יהוה אזמרה

Contents

Introduction

       This book is personal, political, and religious all at once.

Most of all, it is communal and collective. Every book emerges from a long dialogue/wrestle with friends, comrades, and enemies; but the dialogue/wrestle behind this one has been deeper, more intense, than any that I, at least, have been involved in before.

The book was really born when people began to call and write me to say that the *Freedom Seder* had reawakened some sense of Jewishness in them. By doing that, they turned my hesitant sense of my own "private" reawakened Jewishness into a sense that there was a Jewish *People* stirring in some new and unexpected ways. The book was half-written when a leading Jewish magazine called me a self-hating anti-Semite, and I had to take time off to deal with that—politically, and in my own head and spirit. (To tell a secret: I felt miserable and ashamed for four days, until Rebbe Shlomo Carlebach came to The Fabrangen to celebrate with us, and I found myself high on Shabbas song and dance among my *chevra*. Then I suddenly realized I was indeed a free Jew, and the attacks were really not true—and therefore really didn't matter.) On the day I finished chapter V I found myself wearing a cap and realized that, all unconscious, I had put one on because *that* chapter was really Torah-study.

The communality of the book grows in part from a deep and warm involvement with my *chaverim* and *chaverot* of the radical Jewish movement, all of whom have taught me through their action and involvement. It also grows in part from an open dialogue with Jews in

7

general—friendly and hostile—and with some Marxists, anarchists, and Christians who have a strong sense of the importance of Jewish thought and a strong sense of the Jewish component in their own thought.

Because the book is at the same time "mine" and not mine, because it emerges especially from my loving, arguing dialogue with other members of Jews for Urban Justice in Washington, and because the theory laid out in the book is integrally connected with actions that take place outside the book, I have done something strange with its structure: Every chapter (except the last) is immediately followed by a sheaf of actions/celebrations called an *Avodah*. That Hebrew word means both "labor" and "religious service" in the same way that "liturgy" meant originally "the work of the people." Some of these *avodot* were communal religious liturgies, some were public statements or calls to action, some were action memoranda or proposals within the radical Jewish movement. Thus all were "works," "services," or "labors." I agree with some of them and disagree with some, but I have put them where they are because I think all of them may help illuminate the theory or experience laid out in the preceding chapter.

The book begins with my own awakening to Judaism and my wrestlings with the Jewish communities in America and Israel; continues with my understanding of the politico-religious situation of the world-wide Jewish People at this moment in its history; and ends with my sense of the profound religious crisis that we face.

But the book is not finished.

The reason there are no *avodot* after the last chapter is that no "works" have yet been created that help me to understand the last chapter. Together we must create them.

The book therefore ends not with *avodot* but with the ancient rabbinical injunction, "Go and study," and with suggestions of how and where and with whom to study. These injunctions are directed to me as much as any other reader. When Passover came in 1968, I had practically no training or reading at all in Torah or the Jewish tradition. Since then I have studied a great deal, but I do not feel myself to be one learned in the tradition. In that sense, too, the book is not finished: I do not expect to know or believe three years from now what I know and believe now, any more than I have been frozen for the last three years. It is through both *avodot* and study that I expect to learn.

I have listed in the pages called "Going and Studying" the people whose arguments with me about this book suggest to me they would be good for others to "study" with. I thank them. I also thank four people without whose dedicated secretarial and administrative help the book would not exist: Frankie Cox, Nancy Firman, Gretchen Matthews, and Tina Smith. And finally, there are some people with whom it is not so much a matter of "thanking for" or "learning from" as it is "being with": Sharon Rose, Mike Tabor, Donald Jewell, Marc Raskin, and Shoshana, David, and Irene Waskow.

March 31, 1971   — A I W
5 Nisan 5731

From Jewish Radical
to Radical Jew

I

From Jewish Radical to Radical Jew

In the spring of 1968, the Passover celebration of the Liberation from Pharaoh fell on April 12. It was the one element of Jewish ceremony that had survived in my family: survived in my imagination and my wife's, survived to impress with its solemnity my four-year-old son, to puzzle with its bustle my one-year-old daughter, to entrance them both with the oddly crackling matzah.

But in 1968 our spirits were heavy, celebration seemed difficult. Just a week before, a United States Army jeep had been stationed at the foot of our block in midtown Washington, with a machine gun pointing at us and our neighbors. We were still under military occupation. To hold the Seder "under military occupation"—the words kept running through my head—seemed a strangely alien act. To walk down 18th Street past each knot of silent soldiers awoke a dozen images from the Exodus: Martin Luther King invoking the memory of Moses, speaking of standing on the mountain top, gazing into the Promised Land, imagining his death before he could enter—and dying the next day. . . . Burned-out stores, emptied of food and watches and shoes as the Israelites looted Egypt of its gold and jewels before they left, as reparations for four centuries of slavery. . . . Just two weeks before, the Pharaoh in the White House had abdicated under pressure from the people—and we had gone to dance and sing like Miriam, in Lafayette Park across the street. . . . Some of the soldiers who were stationed in our city had been stationed in Hue and Danang not long before. How must it feel there, to be under foreign occupation? And under napalm?

Suddenly knowing that they *were* the Pharaoh's Army

11

. . . and I was a Jew about to celebrate the liberation of my people and the liberation of the Blacks and the liberation of the Vietnamese, from Pharaoh. Not yet. But soon.

Walking home to write a few words to add to the Haggadah I was to read that night: words about an America of Pyramids.

And finding myself more deeply stirred by what I was reading and celebrating, by the Bitter Herb of slavery I shared with my family and the Unleavened Bread of hasty liberation, than by all the efforts at medical relief and legal aid and political protest and public mourning that I had undertaken as an American radical during the previous week. Astounded to discover that being Jewish stirred me, astounded to discover that I had both something to learn from and something to add to the Jewish tradition.

Almost two months later, I was sitting in a meeting of the Urban Affairs Subcommittee of the Jewish Community Council. I had not been asked, and had not gone, out of any strong sense of my Jewishness; I was there because I had written a book on race riots, and now race riots were by far the chief "urban affair" exercising the subcommittee.

But the meeting was interrupted by an emergency phone call from the Poor Peoples Campaign, then haunting Washington from its rickety tents in Resurrection City on the Mall. A new contingent of Poor People had just arrived, but no space was ready for them at Resurrection City. A Catholic church had offered sleeping space, but had no showers for the weary, dirty travelers. The Campaign had asked the nearby Jewish Community Center to make its showers available. The Center had said no. Could the Council do anything?

The subcommittee became a hubbub. Everyone agreed that the Center's behavior was immoral, or stupid, or both. Most of the members were horrified at the denial of a Jewish tradition of hospitality to the poor that, as some muttered, goes all the way back to Abraham's welcoming a batch of scroungy wayfarers. A few were shocked to think of the anti-Semitism among Blacks that the refusal might easily engender. Almost everyone went scurrying off to telephone the big *machers* on the Center board who could make its staff reverse their decision.

But some of us didn't know any *machers*, or didn't think that was the way to get things done anyhow. We clustered into a little circle and began to work out what we could do. It was one thirty. We decided to call our friends—we thought we could easily turn out about fifty people—and show up at the Center at five o'clock. We would give the Center until five thirty to turn on the showers. If they didn't, we would take over the building in the name of the Jewish tradition and the Jewish community, invite the Poor Peoples Campaign to send its people over, and turn on the showers ourselves.

The chief bureaucrat of the Community Council stood there listening to our little band working out our plans . . . stood there listening and wringing his hands. He began to imagine disastrous headlines in the *Washington Post*. Finally he spoke to the oldest among us, a vigorous liberal with a solid reputation for sanity even among the officials of the Jewish Establishment. "Arnold," he said, "I understand how you feel. I even agree with you. But why five thirty? We're making the phone calls right now. I'm sure we can get them to change their minds, but it will take a little time. Why don't you set the deadline for tomorrow morning instead?"

Whereupon Arnold Sternberg answered *not* what I expected—some tag line out of the liberal rhetoric, like "Blacks in America have waited long enough," or something out of common sense, like "They've traveled a long way and they need to shower now, not tomorrow."

Instead he answered, "Because Maariv"—the evening prayer—"is at five thirty, and I intend to *davven* Maariv in the lobby of the Jewish Community Center. *That's* why."

The answer shattered the bureaucrat. How could he,

whose very life was the measuring out of Jews with coffee spoons, deal with such a ridiculous, irrational response? He stood there silent, gasping, and then turned to make the calls that warned the Center of our crazy plan, the calls that made the Center reverse its decision by mid-afternoon in order to forestall us.

So Arnold's answer "won." It shattered the bureaucrat, it shattered the Center. But more important to me, it shattered *me*. That this crazy piece of Jewish tradition, boiling up out of the unconscious and the irrational, could fuse itself with the politics I understood; that my focus as a radical on direct action for life against or around the deadly institutions could find its way against or around in such an utterly Jewish path—this stunned me. Or un-stunned me.

Twice in two months. I found myself half rationally deciding I had better look into this business of Jewishness and religion, half nonrationally driven, tugged to work out a piece of myself that I had barely known existed.

When I started looking carefully at the "religious question," it became clear that something remarkable was happening among young Americans. Religion had become not only an arena of insurgency but a *form* of insurgency. It was not merely a matter of young Catholics raising questions about illegitimate authority in the Church, just as young Democrats were raising questions about illegitimate authority in the Party. It ran deeper than that. People like Allen Ginsberg were trying to exorcise the Pentagon as well as besiege it. People like the Bread and Puppet Theater were handing home-baked bread around between the actors and the audience, in a kind of communion service before doing a radical political theater piece. People like an Episcopal Bishop were holding Mass among bleeding, crying students at Grant Park during the Chicago upheaval. People like Father Dan Berrigan were celebrating a new religious ceremony: burning the records of the Selective Service System. Precisely on the Left, where for a century the automatic dogma had been that religion was the opiate of the people, religion had been turned from a narcotic into an awakener. My own inward experiences during the spring of 1968 were not idiosyncratic; I was sharing them with scores of thousands of other Americans.

Including young Jews. For many of the same Jewish students and young professionals who were filled with fury by the American War against Vietnam and by institutionalized American racism also felt deprived by the operations of American society of the spiritual depth, the communal sense, the traditional rootedness, and the connection between intellect and feeling that were among the best products of Jewish religion, culture, and peoplehood. Many were discovering that these senses are extremely important to them, and perhaps especially so in a civilization that seems hypercerebral.

It occurred to some of them that it is precisely at the end of 250 years of "scientific" (i.e., cerebral and technological) effort that Humanity stands at the point of exterminating itself and—even if we avoid that catastrophe —of poisoning and polluting the world.

Would it be too much to expect that sane people would turn away from such a world, recoil from worship of the technology that created it as from Moloch, and search for roots of prescientific thought and feeling—especially feeling—that might connect them to a sense of mankind and of nature once again? To a sense of love, joy, and community that might color or transform the use of the technology that science made available?

In this fashion these young Jews begin to connect these rulers who decree war, and profit from racism, with the rulers who manage and advance the dehumanized technology. And then to connect and fuse their own opposition, their own resistance.

In that way their "religious" sense—that is, their urgency for reconnecting mind, body, and spirit—becomes not only a "morally" human response to a morally dehumanizing society, but also a "politically" liberating response to politically oppressive institutions. Naturally, in that response there might emerge some very peculiar notions of what religion should be. Indeed, the more "forbidden" a religious expression, the more scornfully it is treated by conventional society, the more attraction it begins to hold for the desperate and the furious young as a form of resistance to the conventionally celebrated death of man. And so some young people began to experiment with astrology and magic as religious insurgencies.

But some began to reexamine the old faiths for new meaning. In the individual biographies of those who are now experimenting with and experiencing the religious impulse, the years of childhood probably determine what form it takes. For some, there are explicit religious rituals and intense communal and family feeling built around them. Then perhaps come years in high school and college during which these feelings of mystery and transcendence are buried and ignored, and the rituals rejected and scorned, in behalf of highly "rational," intellectualized, manipulable science, mathematics, and social science. Then comes the attempt to "transcend MIT" by recovering and retranslating the childhood roots into an adult fusion of intellect and mystery.

Jews who were children in the 1930s and 1940s may have had an especially strong exposure to specifically religious teachings, as their parents reacted to the Holocaust, and may also have had an especially strong dose of the MIT culture, drawing as it does on some particular and partial roots of the Jewish culture. Thus the reaching among Jews for a reintegration of thought and feeling and for a revitalization of Judaism is probably especially strong. And as they look out from their own lives to the social system, their personal biographies and social history seem to recapitulate and strengthen each other, with the last two centuries playing for Mankind as a whole the role of "the years at MIT."

But these "reawakened Jews" are not likely to be

satisfied with conventional Judaism. They will reject precisely those forms of "religion" that are endorsed by,
indeed encouraged by, those who rule the society—such
as prayer breakfasts, such as "Judeo-Christian" dedication
services, such as the tolerated pluralism of marginally
different denominations together with punishment for
radically different faiths like Jehovah's Witnesses, Black
Muslims, the Neo-American Church. Such reawakened
Jews will be looking for religious forms that fuse their
urgency about social change with expressions of spiritual
urgency, that fuse adult concerns for both justice and
community.

The process of rediscovery is not easy. During 1968 and
1969, as I began to wrestle with my own Jewishness, I
learned that in Washington there were already people who
had come out of the civil rights movement in 1966 to
create "Jews for Urban Justice"—an amalgam of aca-
demics, civil servants, lawyers, doctors, and loose-jointed
activists in their twenties or early thirties. They had
formed JUJ in response to two almost simultaneous events:
the urging of the early Black Power movement that whites
go organize their own communities, and the insistence of
a Washington rabbi that religion had nothing to do with
the business behavior of one member of his congregation
who insisted on keeping her apartment house lily-white.
Most of JUJ's members had been so ill-taught by the conventional Jewish institutions that they had little detailed
knowledge of their tradition—a circumstance that first
made them feel guilty and later, as they began to learn its
richness, made them feel angry at the conventional Jewish
community that had failed to teach it to them. A few,
however, had been better taught—one, indeed, came out of
a Chasidic background by way of the Nazi concentration
camps to a strongly Jewish radicalism. And all of them had
a gut sense that the rabbi *must* be wrong, the Judaism that
they vaguely knew surely did have something to say about
racism and money. So JUJ began surveying the social-
action practices of Washington synagogues, leafleting their

services, picketing a Jewish grocery-chain owner who insisted on selling California grapes despite the farm-worker's strike and boycott.

It was indeed the grape boycott that made possible for JUJ an opening to the liveliness of the Jewish tradition. The Boston Board of Rabbis heard solemn testimony on labor conditions in the California grape fields and ruled that California grapes fell under the Talmudic law of *oshek*: the fruit of exploited labor is not lawful food for eating. When that word trickled down to Washington, the reaction of JUJ was relief and disbelief, puzzlement and joy. The Talmud could speak on the issue of the grape strike? Then surely JUJ's vague hunch and hope had been correct, and Judaism was real when it came to politics and to the issues that young Jews cared about.

From then on, JUJ changed more and more speedily from a group of tentatively Jewish young radicals to a group of radically committed Jews who leaped over their own immediate past, leaped over the conservatism and conventionality of their Americanized Jewish upbringing, by appealing to the many strands of intransigent radicalism woven in the older Jewish tradition. Its members discovered that I was wrestling with the Passover Haggadah and had begun to work out a Freedom Seder that drew on my feelings of April 12, 1968. They greeted that kind of work joyfully, convinced me the idea was not my private craziness, made my individual agony communal, and then suggested the Freedom Seder be made a community event.

In 1969 the third night of Passover fell on April 4—the anniversary of King's death and of the nation-wide Black uprising. In the basement of a church in the Black community of Washington, eight hundred people gathered to mourn King and celebrate the fierce love of freedom that bursts forth in every generation of human history, and that in our day and on our continent was fiercest in the Black community and among the anti-war youth.

Why were they responding to the Seder? (Leaving

aside for a moment why the Freedom Seder, and thinking about the vigor of the old Passover.) Not only for its content, the song of liberation that fuses "politics" and "religion." Not only for its occasion, the resonance of times and places, which echoed King for Moses and Uprising for the Plagues. Not only for its focusing of a People through its families, the centrality of children to the Seder and therefore the emotion/intensity of the Seder to adults whose warmest childhood memories it reawakened. But also, and perhaps most basic, for its form: the fusion of word and food, therefore of spirit and body, therefore of ideology and action. In its one moment, a crystal of the unalienated community of unalienated persons.

And a Freedom Seder? It made explicit two strands that have traditionally been implicit in the Seder, and because they have only been implicit have at least recently been thought by most conventional celebrants not to be there at all: the Seder's ability to grapple with contemporary issues of liberation, and the Seder itself as a liberating rather than a hierarchical ceremony. On the first matter, the traditional Seder includes a rabbinical disputation as to whether there were ten, fifty, or one hundred Plagues; the Freedom Seder takes that particular dispute as a kind of symbol of the desirability of disputing, and substitutes for it a dialogue from Jefferson, Thoreau, the Warsaw Ghetto, Buber, Cleaver, and the Berrigans on violence and nonviolence as methods in the struggle. On the second matter, it has always been theoretically acceptable to interrupt and argue, to read additional material into the Haggadah, etc.; but in practice few celebrants did. In the Freedom Seder, time is specifically set aside for "talking back," arguing through the issues.

But it was not enough for the Seder to be constantly contemporary and constantly free. There was a crucial matter of content. The Freedom Seder tried to develop the liturgy in ways that asserted the liberation of the Jewish People *alongside* the liberation of the other peoples—not theirs as against ours, or ours as against theirs. Thus is celebrated the Warsaw Ghetto Uprising of 1943 (Ringelblum) *alongside* the Black Uprisings of the 1960s (King and Cleaver); the liberation of the Jews *alongside* the liberation of the Vietnamese; Rabbi Tamaret on nonviolence *alongside* Gandhi and Berrigan. Some Jews have called the Freedom Seder anti-Semitic. To me it seems that could only be asserted by someone who believed that the liberation of the Jewish and other peoples is incompatible; that celebrating the liberation of Blacks and Vietnamese *ipso facto* means opposing the liberation of Jews; that self-hatred is the inevitable result of loving others.

For the Freedom Seder is neither simply universalist nor simply particularist. Unlike the Christian Mass, which grew out of the Passover, the Freedom Seder does not dissolve all Jewish history in a universal liturgy. It is instead what might be called "multi-particularist," following the form and content of the Seder of Exodus, and then showing how that history has a universally particular meaning—how, indeed, it is appealed to explicitly by Muste and King in their own lives and work. Thus the Freedom Seder is one experimental effort—there have been and will be others—toward what the tradition calls the Passover of the Messianic Age, the Passover of the liberation of all the nations. But the nations when they will still be different from each other—still walking, as Micah says, each in the name of its god.

And so the nations did walk, in miniature, that night in 1969. Black ministers and Black militants, Catholic priests and Left-wing atheists, rabbis and Bundists, that is what the eight hundred did. Shivering as firebells rang in the night outside the church, shivering as they remembered the pall of smoke over Washington the previous year, they wrestled with their fear, talked about the meaning of the slain first-borns of Egypt, talked about the present and future of Judaism and of America. They laughed again over the homely Pesach jokes about the wine, the horseradish, gasped at the question "Why do the Jews think they're so special?" cried as a reader's voice shook over King's last words. And ended both more Jewish and more radical than when they'd come.

The Seder was the crossroads, not the end, of the path JUJ was taking into the burning bushes of the tradition. In the summer of 1969, JUJ sponsored a Tisha B'Av (Ninth of Av) religious service in memory of the Destruction of the Temple in Jerusalem. But this Tisha B'Av service was not conventional; since the United States was near the climax of its debate over the ABM, JUJ held the service on the steps of the United States Capitol. (The ancient legal prohibition on protest on the Capitol grounds had just been defeated, so this was probably the first formal service-of-protest ever held there, and certainly the first Jewish service.) JUJ fused the traditional reading of Jeremiah's Lamentations for Jerusalem with a new mourning over the impending destruction by thermonuclear war of the Temple of Mankind. As Jeremiah thundered that the Temple had been wrecked because the kings of ancient Israel and Judah leaned on military power rather than walking in the path of social justice and religious commitment, so JUJ warned that the obliteration of Washington and the world was being prepared by America's obsession with military might and its rejection of the Prophetic command to seek justice.

The spreading radical Jewish movement developed further its fusion of "religious" celebration and "political" radicalism through the fall and winter of 1969–1970. On Kol Nidre night, at the beginning of Yom Kippur, Jewish communities all over the world gather to confess their sins, express repentance for them, and seek redemption for a life of peace and joy during the succeeding year. Most of them feel it to be the most solemn and poignant moment of the year. On Kol Nidre of 5730, mid-September of 1969, Jews for Urban Justice gathered at a Washington synagogue, at the invitation of its rabbi and board, to participate in and help lead a special service oriented to the younger families among its members and to visiting students. JUJ wrestled with the meaning of the Yom Kippur fast day, and focused on the passage of Isaiah traditionally recited that day: "Is not this the fast that I have chosen? . . . To let the oppressed go free, give thy bread to the hungry, bring the homeless to thy house?"

Out of that examination, JUJ suggested one change in the prayer service: an addition to the Al Chet, the recitation of sins that the congregants have committed during the previous year. One of the verses of the Al Chet runs, "For the sin which we have committed before Thee by violence, and for the sin which we have committed before Thee by profanation of Thy name . . . For all these, O God of forgiveness, forgive us, pardon us, grant us atonement." Out of this verse JUJ proposed to develop a longer statement of the ways in which as *social* beings, not simply as individuals, all Americans in 1969 were participating in murder and idolatry: through participation in their government's war against the people of Vietnam, through participation in their institutions' racism and exploitation of the poor, through the destruction of the environment. The new statement of contrition was to be followed by a communal commitment to act to end the violence, in accordance with the tradition that atonement for sins against God could be accomplished by heart-felt grief, but in regard to sins against human beings only by active restitution.*

Despite the hope of the synagogue's leadership that more conservative members would stay in the purely conventional service being held at the same time, some conservatives insisted on watching the JUJ-influenced service. When the additional prayer was read, some of the conservatives charged forward, tried to stop the service by physical force, and were stopped only by the locked arms and nonviolent stance of some of the celebrants. One of them, a leading Washington slumlord and a major contributor to the congregation, shrieked, "I paid for this

* See "Avodah Aleph," following this chapter.

synagogue, and this is never going to happen in this synagogue again." After the service was continued and completed, and for weeks afterward, JUJ was told that the political views they had expressed would have been easy to discuss if they had been presented any other night than Kol Nidre or in any other way than prayer. What came clear to JUJ and to many of the sympathetic congregants was that the fusion of religious and political feeling into a single whole—in short, a revivification of the old meaning of the Jewish tradition—carried an enormous emotional charge, was far more explosive and far more productive of spiritual and social change than either religion-in-a-box or politics-in-a-box.

Later in the fall, on the day after the Great Mobilization of 400,000 anti-war people in Washington, radical Jews from around the country gathered at a Jewish movement center. They talked, argued, danced, sang, and prayed through the Friday evening Shabbat celebration. They marched behind a Torah in the throngs on Saturday—a true Shabbat Shalom. And the Jewish movement decided to carry through its own tradition. Remembering the destruction of the Golden Calf and the repeated attacks by the Prophets on such murderous idols as the Baalim and Moloch, the movement decided in a large communal discussion on Saturday night to create a new liturgy as an expression of resistance to idolatry. Gathering at the White House at noon on Sunday, the movement blew the Shofar—the great Ram's Horn—as a call to struggle against the Idols of the American state—the Idols of Power, War, Wealth, and Technology. Then in succession those assembled joined in smashing the symbols of those Idols—a giant Golden Calf, a toy bomber, several dollar bills, a toy robot. And finally they sounded the Shofar again, as an echo of the coming Messianic Age of peace, justice, and the abandonment of all idolatry. "Sound the great Shofar of our Liberation!" they proclaimed, and then scattered back across the country to translate the liturgy into continued struggle.

The renewed fusion of political radicalism with religious and spiritual celebration came to a climax in a number of Freedom Seders held around the country in the spring of 1970. Four that I took part in, each remarkably different from the others despite the fact that they began with the same text, taught the possibilities of a renewed Judaism to thousands of young Jews.

The first was held in the Cornell University Field-house the Friday evening before Passover began, as the initial event in a weekend of celebration and support for the radical Catholic priests, Fathers Dan and Phil Berrigan, and for the rest of the draft-resistance movement. Dan Berrigan had been a Cornell chaplain; teachers and students knew and loved him, and some of them had through him begun to honor and join the radical-nonviolent movement. When the weekend had originally been planned, it had been expected that the Berrigans would have started serving Federal jail sentences for their nonviolent destruction of conscription records. But three weeks before, the Berrigans had gone underground—announcing that they considered the law under which they had been sentenced to be immoral, and were now nonviolently resisting that too.

As the Freedom Seder began on April 17, the Berrigans' whereabouts was unknown. Federal agents had been quizzing and following their friends at Cornell and in the town of Ithaca. Three or four thousand students had congregated in the Cornell Field-house. Copies of the service, small plates of matzah and horseradish, cups of wine, were scattered for communal use around the arena. A "head table" of readers—radical students, a couple of Catholic priests, a Jewish draft resister, anti-war professors, a close friend of Dan Berrigan—had begun to recite the ancient invocations for the Feast of Unleavened Bread: "Lo! This is the bread of affliction which our ancestors ate in the land of Egypt. Let all who are hungry eat thereof; and all who are in need and in danger come and celebrate the Passover." As a symbolic door to the Field-house was opened, the readers continued, "As our door is open, may not only the hungry come but also the spirit of the prophet Elijah . . ." And as the reading continued, Dan Berrigan emerged from the clusters of murmuring students, climbed the steps to the "head table," and joined the celebrants.

When the assembly realized what had happened, the Seder paused. Thousands began to laugh and cry. Hundreds came forward to form a living barrier around the head table so that it would not be possible for the Federal agents in the hall to arrest Berrigan. The word went out over campus radio and from mouth to mouth that Berrigan had surfaced. Thousands more students arrived to pack the Field-house and celebrate the Seder.

As the reading reached the passage in the Freedom Seder of discussion and debate on the issues of non-violence and violence as means of liberation, Berrigan joined in as reader and as discussant. As the posing of the issues grew more poignant, he set forth his own situation: should he now voluntarily surrender to the Federal police, or should he vanish again, keep writing and occasionally speaking, continue to argue for nonviolent resistance to the government? Would those present lend him their love and their support—if necessary, their help —if he returned to the underground? The Field-house thundered: told him *Yes,* urged him to stay free.

When the Seder ended, several hours later, he did.

For those of us who had shaped the Freedom Seder, it was a moment of pure joy: the Seder, that festival of remembered liberation, had itself liberated a human being, kept him safe from the Imperial police, let him join in a debate of the deepest moral, religious, and political issues facing us. And not a single human being alone: for it had liberated us along with him.

But the joy was for but a moment. The next night of the Cornell festival I wandered among the crowds in the Field-house baffled, angry, and depressed. The festival of liberation had become a rock concert. The music was liberating, the people were happily dancing, but some hunger gnawed at me. And finally I recognized the hunger:

I missed the Bitter Herb. The Bitter Herb of slavery: slavery recalled, slavery tasted, slavery pressed in on every nerve ending of bitterness, revulsion, fury. The Bitter Herb of the burning Vietnamese children, the flaming stacks of Selective Service records. With Berrigan the convict and the Bitter Herb, with the crackling matzah of a troubled, hasty struggle, the Seder had elevated pleasure to a sublime joy. Joy in Berrigan free and the People's Power and the Spirit that moved the waters.

That night I faced the choice between the Woodstock Nation and the Jewish People, and I learned that thirty-five hundred years of struggle, of knowing that the wine of freedom must be accompanied by the Bitter Herb, had more to teach me than the plunge into Now. In that night, and the few weeks following, I crossed the frontier from being a committed Jewish radical, to being a committed radical Jew.

The next several nights were ways of reexperiencing the Seder from many angles. In New York City we celebrated it on a chilly afternoon at Battery Park, in the shadow of the Pyramids of Wall Street. We reminded ourselves of a dozen ways in which the Rockefeller Empire and its Chase Manhattan Bank oppressed the Jewish People and half the world beside, we remembered the Warsaw Ghetto Uprising alongside people of the older Jewish Left whose movements had fought there during Passover in 1943, and we ended the Seder in a transport of warmth as Shlomo Carlebach led us singing, dancing into a sense of immediate love and liberation.

In Washington we made the mistake of totally "decentralizing" the Seder, so that its physical focus dissolved into a shuffle of vaudeville acts and its political focus into petty argument, but then we pulled it all together again with a magnificent March Against the Pharaohs—a march to the White House and the Soviet Embassy, to protest against the repression of political opposition in both countries, against Soviet anti-Semitism and American racism. At the White House we chanted and reenacted the first nine Plagues—pouring blood on the fence, releasing cockroaches and rats onto the front lawn—as we explained why the Presidency was now Pharaonically oppressive. And then, as we turned to march up 16th Street to the Soviet Embassy and found ourselves facing solid ranks of policemen, and ten blocks of sealed-off city, we danced and sang as the Jews of Moscow do in *their* assertions of the Tradition against state power.

Finally, as Passover was ending and the nation was drawing uneasy breath before the political hurricanes of May, I traveled to New Haven to share in a much more intimate, conversational Seder. Yale University was poised upon moral, political, perhaps even physical, disaster. Tens of thousands of radicals were planning to join on May Day in New Haven to demand the release of all political prisoners, and specifically a group of Black Panthers who were soon to stand trial in New Haven. Threats against Yale had been heard. Some Yale faculty and students had themselves demanded that Yale as an institution support the Panthers and the May Day demonstration. The University was "on strike" when I arrived, and knots of deeply concerned students and teachers were debating, organizing, leafleting, working, to prepare for May Day.

Some students and a rabbi at Hillel, the Jewish student organization, had decided that the Freedom Seder was appropriate to their situation. Forty or fifty of us gathered in a quiet room, huddled together on cushions and the floor, passed a box of matzahs and a jug of wine around the circle, began to meet each other, talked about the strike. And finally, a little awkwardly, began the Seder . . . and slowly relaxed as we stopped to drink the wine, laughed a bit, settled into the rhythm of reading in succession round the circle instead of hearing from one Reader, shared the Haggadahs we were reading from, got deeper into the meaning of the words. Began to see how directly they could teach us. As we reached the discussion of violence and nonviolence the quotations on the page—Jefferson and Cleaver, Ringelblum and Buber—were put aside and people began to talk. If our commitment was to freedom for the Panthers, what did violence mean? Was it necessary? Was it disastrous? *Was* our commitment to freedom for the Panthers? Were they violent? Was the State?

In New Haven that night and all that week there were dozens, hundreds, of such conversations. I doubt that any were more serious, more loving, more open, more careful than this one—conducted in the context of the thirty-five hundred years of Jewish history, Jewish striving, Jewish doubt.

My rediscovery at Cornell of the Bitter Herb and, with it, of elements in the Jewish tradition that I could not learn from modern radicalism, together with my experience in New Haven of the Freedom Seder on a "human scale" rather than a heroic one, helped spur me to the next step in my work to fuse my own celebration with my own liberation. I felt that I had a deeper understanding of the problem, in that I began to see the round of weekly, daily life—not just the special moments of the Holy Days—as the arena for that fusion.

Through the summer and fall of 1970, we in Jews for Urban Justice began to wrestle with Shabbat. Slowly, slowly, a cluster of people began to join and grow around the welcoming of Shabbat at Friday evening communal services—services held not in the rigid rows of suburban synagogues, but in the crowded circle of a living room, by people sitting on cushions on the floor. Services in which our liturgy treated Buber and Fromm and Heschel as seriously as our forefathers' liturgy treated Maimonides in *Yigdal*. Services that women took part in as freely and joyously as men. Services of singing and dancing.

Slowly, slowly, those of us who had been "political" but had been cut off from the "religious" tradition began to understand the "political" dimension of the Shabbat as foretaste of the Messianic Age—Shabbat as a present moment of the future "revolution." More important, we began to experience in our own lives the sense of peace, completeness, community, created by a Shabbat communally celebrated—and therefore to understand more deeply what the "revolution" was that we were seeking. And we began to experience more richly the "religious" significance of the moment out of time.

Avodah Aleph

I—Addition to the Al Chet
Used on Kol Nidre 5730—September 21, 1969
By Jews for Urban Justice

THE CONFESSION

For the sin which we have committed before Thee by violence,
And for the sin which we have committed before Thee by the profanation of Thy name;
For these, O God of forgiveness, forgive us, pardon us, grant us atonement.

O Lord our God, King of the Universe!

Hear our sins that we have sinned together, in unholy union:

We have sinned by killing other human beings—

By paying soldiers to burn Vietnamese babies alive— *without forcing our rulers to stop the war machine;*

By sending 40,000 of our sons to be killed in an illegal war—*without forcing our rulers to stop the war machine;*

By using chemical products that poison the air and give people cancer—ourselves and our families included— *without forcing our rulers to change these products;*

By using machines for transportation that are so built that they club, slash, and mutilate people—ourselves and our families included—

without forcing our rulers to change these machines;

By creating and using a medical system that condemns black babies to die at twice the rate of white and Jewish babies—

without forcing our rulers to change the medical system;

By creating, owning, and supporting a system of grocery stores that starves some children into apathy and death while we and our children get fat—

without forcing our rulers to feed all children, free;

By paying and applauding policemen who gas, shoot, and beat Black people and our own children—

without forcing our rulers to place the police under the control of the people they police;

By keeping Black people out of our neighborhoods, and not keeping rats out of the Black neighborhoods, so Black children are bitten to death by rats—

without forcing our rulers to end the existence of slums.

So in all these ways

We have murdered, O Lord;

We have killed real children;

We ourselves have done it,

And we have allowed others to do it while we turn our eyes away;

For some of us are physicians, and murder;

And some of us are grocers, and murder;

And some of us own real estate, and murder;

And some of us drive automobiles, and murder;

And some of us use pesticides, and murder;

And some of us serve on draft boards, and murder;

And all of us pay taxes—for murder.

Nor have we here today redeemed ourselves before our sisters and brothers—

For although we dare offer atonement to Thee today,

We have not gone to those whose brothers, sisters, and children we have murdered, to redress our crimes.

And we have not gone to our rulers

To force them to end their crimes.

For they are even more responsible than we, since they
   have more power,
And even more irresponsible than we, for they use it
   worse.
Instead of stopping them,
We have respected them;
Instead of tearing down the idols they erected,
We have worshipped at their obscene shrines.
We have acted as though Presidents were Kings,
Although You are the only King we have.
So we confess before Thee
Not only murder, but idolatry.
Not only murder, but apostasy.
Not only murder, but the profanation of Thy name.

THE VOW

O Lord, We know that we must *act*
In order to win forgiveness.
We have searched our hearts
And we are ready to act.
Today is a day You named for us to fast from food;
We shall name for ourselves a day to fast from sin.
Let us appoint a day, as Isaiah tells us,
To remove oppression from our midst,
To bestow our bread on the hungry,
To relieve the afflicted soul.
We shall join with the others of our country
Who have chosen October 15 for that day.
And on that day we shall do no work,
But we shall gather here to plan:
How to end the war that afflicts our people;
How to end the colonial status of our city;
How to end the destruction of our air and water.
And on that day we shall gather no money,
But we shall give our pay to the organized poor—
To the National Welfare Rights Organization.
And on that day we shall gather our friends

To meet and act with us.

O Lord, help Thou our effort!

These vows we make in solemn assembly;

These vows we make with joy!

And having made these vows,

We shout to Thee with a glad heart.

For *now*, O God of forgiveness, we are free to ask Thee: forgive us our sins!

For the sin which we have committed before Thee by violence,

And for the sin which we have committed before Thee by the profanation of Thy name,

Now, O God of forgiveness, forgive us, pardon us, grant us atonement!

II—Introduction to a Service of Personal/Political Encounter

On Rosh Hashanah 5731—October 1, 1970 Led by Jews for Urban Justice

Abraham, Abraham!

Yes, O Lord?

Throughout the world there is an outcry against the City of Washington, that their sins are very grievous; and I will go down now, and see whether they have done altogether as the outcry says that has come unto me; and if not, I will know. But if the outcry be true and the sin grievous, then shall I rain brimstone and fire upon that city; and lo, the smoke of that country shall go up as the smoke of a furnace; and I shall overthrow that city, and all its people, and all that grows upon its ground.

Will thou destroy also the righteous with the wicked? Perhaps there be 50 righteous within the city; wilt thou also destroy and not spare the place for the 50 righteous that are therein? That be far from thee to do after this

manner, to slay the righteous with the wicked; shall
not the Judge of all the earth do justly?

If I find in Washington 50 righteous within the city, then
I will forgive all the place for their sake.

Behold now, I have taken upon me to speak unto the Lord,
who am but dust and ashes. Perhaps there shall lack 5
of the 50 righteous; wilt thou destroy all the city for
lack of five?

I will not destroy if I find there 5 and 40.

Perhaps there shall be 40 found there.

I will not do it for the 40's sake.

Oh, let not the Lord be angry, and I will speak. Perhaps
there shall be 30.

I will not do it if I find 30 there.

Behold now, I have taken upon me to speak unto the
Lord. Perhaps there shall be 20 found there.

I will not destroy it for the 20's sake.

Oh let not the Lord be angry, and I will speak yet but this
once. Perhaps 10 shall be found there.

I will not destroy it if there are but ten. *Show me the ten.*

(Followed by open discussion and personal prayer.)

III—Introduction to a Service of Encounter
On Kol Nidre 5731—October 9, 1970
Led by Jews for Urban Justice

Jonah, Jonah!

Yes, O Lord?

Arise, go to America, that great city, and preach unto it
the preaching that I bid thee, for their wickedness is
come up before me.

What shall I preach?

Cry against America: Yet 40 days, and America shall be
overthrown.

But they will repent, and turn; and then thou wilt forgive

them and my journey be for nought; for I know thou
art a gracious God, and merciful.

If they repent, shall your journey be for nought? If they
turn every one from his evil way, and from the violence
that is in their hands, shall your journey be for nought?

But the journey is thirsty, the preaching is thirsty, and my
soul is thirsty. And America will have no water for my
thirst; for they are not of the House of Jacob, neither
are they the People of thy Law. Wherefore shall I
suffer that they be redeemed?

Shall I leave them to suffer in their sinfulness? Shall I not
be sorry for the great city of America, with its ten score
million people who cannot tell their right hand from
their left, and even for its many many cattle? Are they
not my people, and the work of my hands? Go and
prophesy!

But . . .

Go and prophesy!

(Followed by open discussion and personal prayer.)

*IV—The Day of Revolutionary Tranquillity:
Toward a Radical Shabbat*

All sing: Chesed u-mishpat ashira, l'cha Adonai azamaira
. . . I'daveed mizmor!

(Of love and justice I will sing; to you, O Lord, I'll sing
praises . . . from David, this psalm!)

One person lights two candles, and all recite:

Baruch atah Adonai elohainu melech ha'olam, asher kid'-
shanu b'mitzvotav ve'tzivanu l'hadlik ner shel shabbat.

Blessed art thou, O Lord our God, king of the universe,
who has made us holy with thy commandments and
commanded us to light the Sabbath lights.

May the Lord bless us and protect us; may the Lord make
his face to shine upon us and be gracious to us; may
the Lord lift up his face upon us and grant us peace.

Sing: Oseh shalom.

[If there is a young child in the company, he or she may ask: Why is this night different from all the other nights of the week? On all the other nights we do not light any candles; on this night we do. On all the other nights we drink just milk or coffee or soda; tonight we have wine. On all the other nights we talk without singing; tonight we sing.]

A reader: Tonight is the beginning of Shabbat, when we rest from our regular work, think about what is good and what is bad, share the joy of studying the Torah together, and try to act especially loving toward each other and all other people. All this we do in hope of a time when all days may be like Shabbat—days of peace and justice, freedom and community, love and thought. As our prophet Isaiah taught, "Thus says the Lord: Hold to justice and do right. For my salvation is at hand and soon my Justice will prevail. Happy the one who does this, who holds fast by it: Who keeps the Sabbath by not profaning it, and keeps his hand from doing any evil." We sing because songs are a way for us here to join our different voices into one community; we drink from our wine a joy that our predecessors drew from their vineyards three thousand years ago; we light candles because the Torah's call to freedom lights our way into the future. Shabbat is a time that lives through time: before, and now, and forever.

As we read in the Torah, the Shabbat was doubly created, as both a day of fulfillment and a day of freedom.

First it is written that God created the Shabbat, for himself, as a day of fulfillment: "Thus the heavens and earth were finished and all their host. And by the seventh day he rested from all his work which he had been doing. And God blessed the seventh day and made it holy, because on it God rested from all the work he had been doing in creation."

And then it is written that God created the Shabbat for

us, as a day of freedom: "Observe the Sabbath day and make it holy, as the Lord your God commanded you. Six days shall you labor and do all your work, but on the seventh day, the Sabbath of the Lord your God, you shall do no work, neither you, nor your son, nor your daughter, nor your man servant nor your maid servant, nor your ox, nor your ass, nor any of your cattle, nor the alien who is within your gates, that your man servant and your maid servant may rest as well as you. For you should remember that you were once slaves in the land of Egypt, and that the Lord your God brought you out of there by a strong hand and outstretched arm. That is why the Lord your God has commanded you to observe the Sabbath day."

And most of all, we celebrate this day of tranquillity and freedom because, as our teachers said, to do so is to bring nearer the Days of Peace and Justice: "If the whole community were just once to observe fully two Sabbaths in a row, we would all be redeemed, liberated, at once."

All stand, face toward the door, and sing:

L'cha dodi, l'krat kalah,
P'nai shabbat n'kablah.
L'krat shabbat l'chu v'nailchah,
Ki hi m'kor ha'brachah,
Meh-rosh m'kedem n'suchah,
Sof ma'aseh b'mach'shavah t'chilah.

One opens the door as all recite:

Beloved, come, the bride to meet,
The Queen of Sabbath let us greet.
Come, to the Sabbath greetings bring,
For it is blessing's constant spring;
Of old ordained, divinely taught,
Last in creation, first in thought.
Beloved come, the bride to meet,
The Queen of Sabbath let us greet.

A reader: At the heart of the celebration of the Sabbath as our forerunners shaped it were certain statements of belief and commitment. Some among us believe them still, as they were written; others understand them as searchings in the Way. Let us join in reciting them: Bar'chu et Adonai hamvorach.

All: Baruch Adonai hamvorach l'olam va-ed. Praise ye the Lord, to whom all praise is due. Praised be the Lord to whom all praise is due forever and ever.

All: Shema Yisrael, Adonai elohanu, Adonai echad.
Baruch shem k'vod malchuto l'olam va-ed.
Hear O Israel, the Lord our God, the Lord is One.
Praised be his name whose glorious kingdom is forever and ever.

All read together: You shall love the Lord your God with all your heart, with all your soul, and with all your might. And these words, which I command you this day, shall be in your heart. You shall teach them diligently to your children, speaking of them when you sit in your house, and when you walk by the way, when you lie down, and when you rise up. And you shall bind them for a sign upon your hand, and they shall be for frontlets between your eyes. And you shall write them upon the doorposts of your house, and upon your gates. That you may remember and do all my commandments and be holy unto your God.

And among my commandments: The children of Israel shall keep the Sabbath, to observe the Sabbath throughout their generations, for an everlasting covenant. It is a sign between me and the children of Israel forever.

The reader: Adonai yimloch l'olam va-ed. The Lord shall reign forever and ever—the Lord, and no earthly monarch. As we have freed ourselves from many a monarch, saved ourselves from powers stronger than our own, so may we liberate ourselves again, and so may all others who are oppressed and persecuted. And to that end we celebrate this Sabbath, this day of liberation.

(All meditate in silence for a few minutes.)
All sit down.

A reader: Shabbat is not for today only, nor is it merely a symbol of the days to come. It shares their being, it is a prefiguration of the Days of Peace and Justice. There is a legend:

When God gave the Torah to his people Israel, he said: "My children! If you accept the Torah and observe my commandments, I will give you for all eternity a thing most precious that I have in my possession."

"And what," asked Israel, "is that precious thing thou wilt give us if we obey thy Torah?"

"The world to come."

"But that is still to come. Show us in this world an example of the world to come."

"The Sabbath is an example of the world to come."

Another reader: The sage Heschel tells us, "He who wants to enter the holiness of the day must first lay down the profanity of clattering commerce, of being yoked to toil. He must go away from the screech of dissonant days, from the nervousness and fury of acquisitiveness and the betrayal in embezzling his own life. To sanctify the seventh day does not mean: Thou shalt mortify thyself, but on the contrary: Thou shalt sanctify it with all thy heart, with all thy soul and with all thy senses. 'Sanctify the Sabbath by choice meals, by beautiful garments; delight your soul with pleasure.' The soul cannot celebrate alone, so the body must be invited to partake in the rejoicing of the Sabbath."

Another reader: And the sage Fromm tells us, "The Sabbath symbolizes a state of union between man and nature and between man and man. I can carry a heavy load within my house without violating the Sabbath law. But I must not carry even a handkerchief from one domain to another—for instance, from the private domain of the house to the public domain of the street. 'Work' is not physical effort, but any interference by man with the physical world. 'Rest' is a state of peace between man and nature. Man becomes natural, and nature becomes human. On the Sabbath, man ceases completely to be an animal whose main occupation is to fight for survival and to sustain his biological life. On the Sabbath, man is fully man, with no task other than to be human."

Another reader: The Shabbat is a time that lives through time. As Heschel tells us, "On the Sabbath it is given us to share in the holiness that is in the heart of time. Time is continuous creation. Time is God's gift to the world of space. Eternity utters a day." The Sabbath is a temple not in space, but in time. And the time it partakes of is The End of Days.

All recite: May the time be near, O God, when thy name shall be worshipped in all the earth, when idolatry shall disappear and the false gods of power and wealth be worshipped no more. Fervently we pray that the day soon come when all who dwell on earth shall invoke thy name, when corruption and domination shall give way to justice and freedom, when superstition shall no longer enslave the mind, when all shall know that to thee alone should every knee be bent and every tongue give homage. May all of us, created in thine image, know and feel that we are comrades, brothers, sisters, one in spirit and in fellowship, united before thee. Then shall the kings vanish, and thy kingdom come. Then shall the words of thy Torah be fulfilled: The Lord will reign forever and ever; on that day the Lord shall be One and his name shall be One. Bayom ha-hu yi-h'yeh Adonai echad u'shmo echad.

A reader: When that day comes, it will be an Age of Shabbat—an age of peace, justice, plenty, tranquillity, and joy. Our prophets Micah and Isaiah have described it:

In the last days it shall come to pass that the mountain of the house of the Lord shall be established high above the mountains, and shall be raised high above the hills; and people shall flow unto it.

And many nations shall come, and say, Come, let us go up to the mountain of the Lord, and to the house of the God of Jacob; and he will teach us of his ways, and we will walk in his paths: for the law shall go forth out of Zion, and the word of the Lord from Jerusalem.

And he shall judge among many peoples, and rebuke strong nations afar off; and they shall beat their swords into plowshares, and their spears into pruning hooks; nation shall not lift up sword against nation, neither shall they learn war any more.

But they shall sit every man under his vine and under his fig tree; and none shall make them afraid: for the mouth of the Lord of hosts has spoken.

Then the eyes of the blind shall be opened, and the ears of the deaf unstopped; then shall the lame man leap like a deer, and the tongue of the dumb sing for joy. For waters shall break forth in the wilderness, streams in the desert; the burning sand shall become a pool, and the thirsty ground become springs of water; the haunt of jackals shall become a swamp, the grass shall become reeds and rushes.

The wolf shall dwell with the lamb, and the leopard lie down with the kid, and the calf and the lion and the fatling together; and a little child shall lead them.

The cow and the bear shall feed; their young shall lie down together; and the lion shall eat straw like the ox.

The sucking child shall play over the hole of the asp, and the weaned child shall put his hand on the adder's den.

In that day Israel will be the third with Egypt and Assyria, a blessing in the midst of the earth, whom the Lord of hosts has blessed, saying, "Blessed be Egypt my people, and Assyria the work of my hands, and Israel my heritage."

They shall not hurt or destroy in all my holy mountain; for the earth shall be full of the knowledge of the

Lord as the waters cover the sea.

All sing: Lo yisah goy el goy cherev, lo yilmadu od milchamah.

Another reader: And in our own day the poet Aaron Zeitlin has written of the Age of Shabbat:

When some day all have work and abundance both
A Lenin of all the blind and the lamed
Will take up the cause of the man who is maimed
And become the great Singer of Justice and Truth.
Capital will have been slaughtered by then
But he'll lead the mobs against laboring
As now they are led against Capital.

And thus, the Last International—
International of Man, the Maimed,
Of all the blind and all the lamed,
Of poets who want not to sweat, but to sing,
As they count Sephira, ring by ring
Above unknown waters.

Hark! the Last International's song,
International of the multitudes
Who never yearn, and will never learn,
To be chained to laboring:
A premature anthem—but one could be wrong.

A man will come at the end of days
The Foe of Toil and Care,
Firing up all those who wear
The gold, yet deserve smelting down themselves,
The Nonworkers of the World.
And thus the Last Leader will proclaim:

Work is the Daughter of Capital,
Work is no End; work is a Way,
Only, toward the ultimate Play,
The free, sublime Play for God.

And crowds will wander among the cities,
And among the cities the crowds will cry
Give us happiness
Give us happiness
Give us happiness
Turn backward, turn backward, turn backward, yes,
All joys—hands, feet, eyes,
Paradise!
And the cry will rip through seas and skies
And God Himself must then descend
And assume some shape; in a splendid guise
Of starry and soul-studded robes
He reveals himself
To the Revolutionists.
And the cosmic Boaz will open his store
And of his riches
Give each that which is
His: To the blind, a flaming eye;
To the halting speaker, the sharpest tongue;
To the twisted, the straightness of the oak;
To the poet, the Song as yet unsung;
To every sterile woman, her Child
To every Golem, his human Creator.

This is the song of the ultimate,
Highest and truly just,
International.

All sing: Arise, ye prisoners of starvation;
Arise, ye wretched of the Earth!
For justice thunders condemnation,
A better world's in birth.
No more tradition's chains shall bind us,
Arise ye slaves, no more in thrall!
The world shall rise on new foundations,
We have been nought; we shall be all!
It is the final conflict;

Let each stand in his place.
The international movement
Shall be the human race!

Arise, ye victims of pollution;
Arise, ye poisoned of the Earth!
All life demands a revolution,
A loving world's in birth.

No more tradition's chains shall bind us,
Arise ye slaves, no more in thrall!
The world shall rise on new foundations,
We have been nought; we shall be all!
It is the final conflict;
Let each stand in his place.
The international movement
Shall be the human race!

A reader: And how shall we bring to life the Days of Peace and Justice we imagine? As the sage Fromm tells us, "Not through a magic ritual, but through a form of practice which puts man in a real situation of harmony and peace." Through creating in our own lives now the revolutionary peace we imagine for the future. Through working and struggling six days of the week that the whole community may come to freedom and tranquillity on the seventh. For let us remember: if all of us would just once observe the Sabbath twice in a row, we would all be liberated at once.

The task of resting is not easy. We must struggle to rest, we must struggle to redeem: we must indeed struggle against great odds and overwhelming power—as the tradition tells us by explaining that we must struggle against even the All-Powerful himself:

After Yom Kippur one year the Berditschever Rebbe called over a tailor and asked him to relate his argument with God on the day before. The tailor said: "I declared to God: You wish me to repent of my sins, but I have committed only minor offenses; I may have kept left-over cloth, or I may have eaten without washing my hands.

"But Thou, O Lord, hast committed grievous sins: Thou hast taken away babies from their mothers, and mothers from their babies. Let us be quits: mayest Thou forgive me, and I will forgive Thee."

Said the Berditschever: "Why did you let God off so easily? You might have forced Him to redeem all of Israel!"

Another reader: But no one person can redeem all Humanity. It is a whole generation, a whole community, that must take action. Once, they say, the Maggid of Mezritsh demanded that the redemption come. He was asked from heaven: "Who is he that dares to hasten the End and what does he consider himself?" The Maggid answered, "Since I am the leading zaddik of this generation, it is my duty to contend for the redemption." The voice asked him: "How can you prove that you are the leading zaddik of the generation?" The Maggid replied, "My holy community will come and witness that I am really the leading zaddik of the generation!" Then the voice from heaven said, "If so let your holy community rise up and give witness for you and then you will have proven that you are the zaddik of the generation." The Maggid went to his holy community and when they all sat before him asked them, "Is it true that I am the zaddik of my generation?" But nobody said "Yes" to this question. He asked them three times, and there was not a single person who would answer him.

Another reader: It is our own actions that must bring the Days of Peace and Justice, our whole community that is responsible for its delay. If together we could be wholly just with each other, wholly free, wholly at rest in joy—then the kingdoms would fall and the great Liberation would occur. May it be in our day!

All: May we bring it in our own day!

All recite the Kiddush: Blessed be thou, O Lord our God, King of the Universe, who has made us holy by thy commandments and has been gracious to us and given us in love the heritage of Shabbat. For Shabbat is to us a memorial of the creation, and is also first among the days of holy convocation that recall the Liberation from Egypt. Thou hast brought us near to thy service, and in love and grace given us the Sabbath. Blessed be thou, O Lord, who makes the Sabbath holy. Baruch atah Adonai elohanu melech ha-olam, boray p'ri hagafen. Blessed be thou, O Lord our God, King of the universe, who createst the fruit of the vine. (Drink wine.) Baruch atah Adonai, elohanu melech ha-olam, ha-motzi lechem min haaretz. Blessed be thou, O Lord our God, King of the Universe, who bringest forth bread from the earth. (Eat challah and salt.)

(Eat the Sabbath dinner.

Afterward, read and discuss part of the Torah or Haftarah portion of the week or a Chassidic tale, a passage of Buber, a poem, etc. After this discussion, one member of the group might mention a problem that has concerned him or her during the week and lay it out for discussion by the collective.)

End the celebration by reciting the Kaddish and singing songs:

Glorified and hallowed be the great name of God throughout the world which he has created according to his will. May he establish his kingdom during our life and during our days, and during the life of all the house of Israel, speedily and soon; and say ye, Amen.

May his great name be blessed for all eternity.

Blessed, praised, glorified, exalted, adored, honored, extolled, and lauded be the name of the Holy One, blessed be he, though he be high above all the blessings, hymns, and praises we can utter; and say ye, Amen.

May abundant peace and life descend from heaven upon us, all Israel, and all humanity; and say ye, Amen.

May he who makes peace in his high heaven bring peace upon us, all Israel, and all humanity; and say ye, Amen.

Israel and Zion

II

Israel and Zion

Flashback.

"What's your position on Israel?"

Flashback because in the midst of my wrestling to fuse celebration with liberation in my own life, to re-create a Jewish identity for myself, the question recurred, again and again. Put, suspiciously, by Jews who had no sense of what this strange "new" animal, a radical Jew, could be. (Forgot it wasn't so new an animal. Only new *this* generation, since 1940. Jews without a history . . . Now *that* was new.) Put, harshly, by Leftists who never thought of asking, "How do you *feel* about Israel?"

Impossible to create a Jewish identity without coming to terms with the question.

Flashback also because in the spring of 1969, I went to Israel. Midway between my freakout into being Jewish on the "Uprising Seder" night of 1968 and my freakout into being a Jew on the "Berrigan Seder" night of 1970. Went because my wife wanted to visit her sister, who had lived on a kibbutz for nineteen years.

My own childhood had never included more than a cursory interest in Zionism. (On Pearl Harbor morning, when I was eight years old, I heard the news after coming in from walking the neighborhood, collecting coins in a little blue can acquired in Sunday school, labeled "Jewish National Fund." And in 1948, one of my non-Jewish high school friends talked about volunteering to fight for Israel till her borders stretched from "the Nile to the Euphrates." I thought he was crazy. The two most Zionist moments of my "pre-political" years.) But Irene had learned Yiddish and Hebrew in a Labor Zionist Folkschul in Milwaukee. Her sister had gone further:

worked hard in Habonim, the moderate Labor Zionist youth group, and then gone off to live, marry a Canadian-raised Habonimnik a lot like herself, and have *sabra* children on a kibbutz in the Negev desert. So to Irene Israel was a much stronger reality than it was to me.

Flash forward: I ended up feeling toward Israel about as I would toward a sister-in-law. Not like a wife, not like a sister . . . but something!

And I came to a "position," too: a position in all the formal sense in which Leftists and older Jews demanded one. But the feeling is where the position grew from, and the feeling was rooted in that trip in the spring of 1969.

The trip exists for me less in a connected memory than in a series of flashes, discontinuous moments. But the flashes tend to concentrate: over and over, they involve two kinds of community: the kibbutz and the Orthodox. Few memories of Tel Aviv, or Haifa, or modern Jerusalem; few memories of "normal" Israel.

Abnormal Israel. Communitarian Israel. S'fad. The town of the mystics for one thousand years: rocky hillsides and alleys painted bright soft blue, tiny schuls of cushions in a horseshoe round the Ark, a transplanted shtetl-worker to explain that here the Holy Rebbe washed in the mikveh each time he wrote the name of God upon his Torah, the heavy curtain to screen aside the few wives who came to pray. . . .

Mea Shearim, the ultra-Orthodox quarter of Jerusalem. Puzzled glances at my clothes and beard: what was I? The fathers and their miniature-grown-up sons, walking together seriously, proudly, toward the synagogue. The long-sleeved women staying much closer to their doorways. The warning: if I must drive my car when it was Shabbas, at least take off my yarmulke so no one would think I was one of them. . . .

The Wall. Empty of meaning when it was empty of people on a Thursday afternoon, full-charged with meaning on a Friday evening as dozens of small congregations come to greet the approaching Queen Shabbat. To greet!

—to dance, to sing, to sway, each group with its own melody and ritual, hundreds of joyful men reaching to touch the Wailing Wall, wheeling to see the Shabbat in as the sun dipped low. Men, only men. And the mournful barrier past which far fewer, lonelier women kept a sadder sort of vigil with the Wall.

And the kibbutz? Equally a community, but with a "heavier" tone, a workers' tone. Of course the Orthodox worked, and of course the kibbutz celebrated; but the Orthodox felt like a community created around the Shabbat and its rest; the kibbutz, a community gathered around the six days of work.

Men and women shivering in the early dawn, pouring out to the orchards to pick the apricots before they could turn from ripe to rotten. The children's farmlet, where goats and vegetables were raised by small kibbutzniks. Walking with the tractor man who last year had been *maskir* and managed the kibbutz, who next year would be a shepherd and tend the lambs.

Joining a kind of new kibbutznik "Shabbat service" focused upon work: the bi-weekly general meeting to make decisions on every area of kibbutz life. Orchardists and the cotton growers arguing out, for all to judge, the amount of irrigation water the two crops needed; the kitchen staff proposing new arrangements for the meals; a school committee reporting on discussions with other kibbutzim about a high school. This "Shabbat" it should be noted, one where men clearly were most authoritative but women were clearly legitimate; where sexual equality was accepted as desirable but not achieved.

Hearing our children shushed for laughing aloud in the communal dining hall. Blinking as a twelve-year-old girl gently turned down the gift of a bikini swimming suit: she would be too embarrassed among her friends to wear it. Listening to an American kibbutznik-in-training bemoan the rigidity and "straightness" of Israelis' fear of marijuana, and hearing from Israelis that "the reason the Arabs lose the wars is that they smoke the stuff."

Hearing every radio in the kibbutz go on for the 10 P.M. news of national politics, the latest death of soldiers and civilians, the latest maneuver in international relations. Carefully explaining the American New Left at a coffee-kumsitz where every instant felt like a loaded mine, where young kibbutzniks sat tensely ready to explode if I rubbed together three words critical of Israel. Visiting the lookout tower and the air-raid shelter—almost shrines.

And sensing what neither the Orthodox nor the kibbutzniks could believe: that they were more like each other than either was like mass-urban Israel; that we could love them both, though they regarded each other with bafflement and sometimes horror. Perhaps the feelings we gathered from a hasty trip were off-key; but, indeed, the kibbutz felt like the shtetl turned inside-out, focused on the work instead of Shabbat, on a common decision of what crops to grow and what food to eat instead of on kashrut, on state politics and the news broadcasts rather than on the Talmud, on total equality of income rather than charity in schul—but still the shtetl. We saw the male domination of the one, the super-patriotism of the other; the subordination of everything to work, in the one, the subordination of everything to prayer, in the other, as problems. But we recognized the wholeness, the unpretentiousness, the sharing of the wealth in goods and spirit that came from both.

And we recognized their Jewishness . . . perhaps because they were still minority cultures, and communities. Perhaps because they were both still emotionally and ideologically connected with the world-wide Jewish People—the one through religion, the other through the Zionist movement. It was much harder to feel Jewishness in the market stalls of Beersheva, in the sophisticated shops of Tel Aviv, in the bus depots of Jerusalem. They felt Israeli, but not especially Jewish (as large parts of suburban "Jewish" Chicago feel American, but not especially Jewish). And that impression—of a new identity that was strongly Israeli but not always strongly involved with the world-wide Jewish People—was reinforced by some of my meetings with political figures. It was crystallized by meeting a maverick member of the Knesset, Uri Avnery. His fierce assertion of Israeliness, alongside his casual disregard for traditional Zionism, confronted in my head the shibboleths about Israel as a Western-Zionist outpost which had already in 1969 become fairly current in parts of the New Left. *Israel Without Zionists*, the title of his book, rattled in my head as an idea—an idea that seemed not quite accurate, but a fruitful error. More important than Avneri's mere personal stance was the excitement and energy he seemed to rouse among a wide swathe of young Israelis—and the hostility he roused from older ones, of left and right, religious and nonreligious. Birth, death, and time seemed to be moving in the direction of more "Israelis" and fewer "Jews."

The discovery that "committed Jews" might come to be a minority among the Israeli population and the discovery that I felt an emotional connection with two quite different kinds of Jewish community in Israel that I did not feel with all Israelis forced me to think more deeply about the philosophical, almost theological, meaning of Israel. (All good philosophy and theology begins with the inner data of human feeling—though it does not end there.) I began to make a distinction between "Israel" and "Zion." "Israel" seemed to be a state like other states, which ought to be treated with as much respect as Sweden or Chile—but no more; a state responsible to an Israeli people, which was entitled to self-determination as were any people, but not entitled to suppress the self-determination of other peoples. "Zion" seemed a much more elusive concept. I kept wanting to apply it to two different things: the Place, as yet unachieved, from which the Prophets tell us the teachings of the Lord will go forth to all the world; and the communities of committed Jews living directly in relation with Eretz Yisrael . . . the land itself. And for the first time I found myself wanting to understand some relation between "the Diaspora," the Dispersion of Jews around the world, and "Zion" in this new sense of the committed Jewish communities in Eretz Yisrael.

The first time I found myself trying to spell out such a notion was on a cool evening high above Jerusalem, eating with a kibbutznik and kibbutz theorist named Dan Leon. I told him perhaps I was a "Diasporanist" as he was a "Zionist." He blinked, said he had never heard of such a thing . . . and I kept talking. I was helped to shape my distinctions because he was an anti-statist, felt deeply (and wrote in his book *The Kibbutz*) that the loose confederation of different political parties and guerrilla armies which fought the War of Independence in 1948, the loose confederation of school systems, labor unions, towns, and settlements which had made up the Yishuv before the proclamation of the state—that this looseness was indeed the genius of the people at its best. He was sad that it had been abandoned to a central state.

Somehow I connected his imagery of the Yishuv with a story from Tanach that had always deeply delighted me: the story of Samuel, Saul, God, and the people of Israel. The people had been living as a confederation of tribes, governed by "judges" who emerged and disappeared as their talents and the needs of the people shifted. But the people came to Samuel: "Appoint us a king to rule over us, like the other nations." God, however, tells Samuel to remind the people: They have a King, their King is the Lord; by demanding a king they are worshipping other gods. "Tell them what sort of king will govern them." And Samuel explains that a king will conscript the young men for war and the young women for his kitchens and bureaucracy; he will take a tenth of the people's grain and flocks—10 percent of the GNP—and make them his slaves. No, said the people; "we will have a king like all the other nations, to lead us out to war and fight our battles." So Samuel and the Lord decide that the people themselves must choose: "Let them have a king, since that is their decision." In short, the higher good is the loose confederacy of kibbutzim and communities; but if the people cannot rise to that level and if it is their will to have a state like all the other nations, then so be it.

So for me there was a partial joining of the two concepts of Zion: the committedly Jewish communities in Eretz Yisrael (one sense of Zion) had embodied the Teaching that night have gone forth to all the earth (the other sense of Zion): the Teaching of community and justice without a state, without a king. Like the people in Samuel's day, they had failed.

Failed because it was not possible, as it had not been possible in Samuel's day to face the Philistines without a king?

Failed because there was no way to build "community and socialism in one country," so long as the other countries were statist and hostile? Failed because the abolition of the state and the creation of community could not happen in isolation in one small area of world politics, and would have to happen as well in the great powers? Failed because such great changes would have to occur in America, and Russia, and France, and Egypt—for them to occur in Israel?

Failed because the creation of the true Zion required the energy of the Diaspora as well—the Diaspora not as a "support group" for Israel, but in its own identity, seeking to transform the world outside of Israel?

These were the kinds of questions my stronger understanding of Israel and the Israelis began to stir into my head.

So from Israel I learned to take the Diaspora more seriously.

That was not all I learned, however. The more seriously I took the existence of an *Israeli* people, the more seriously I took the reports and warnings by some Israelis that there was a Palestinian people too: not "Arab refugees," but a *Palestinian people*. With help from left-wing

Israelis, I was able to arrange a brief visit to several different kinds of Palestinian political figures on the Israeli-occupied West Bank of the Jordan River.

Some of them (like the Sheikh of Hebron) were traditional semi-feudal figures; others, like city councilmen in Bethlehem and a politically active physician in Ramallah, were middle-class nationalists. All agreed that most of the Palestinians did not want to be ruled either by Jordanians or Israelis; all insisted that most of the Palestinians on the West Bank, at least, were prepared to live in peace with Israel; all asserted that the Israeli government had rejected their pleas to allow the emergence of a political voice for Palestinian desires. One described asking for permission to hold a convention of political notables on the West Bank which could choose a quasi-cabinet to negotiate with Israel for Palestinian independence: Permission refused. Another spoke of holding elections, under perhaps a tripartite Trusteeship by Israel, an Arab government, and a neutral state: Proposal rejected. Others spoke of various approaches: all denied.

So they all spoke in tones of despair.

"Look," said one of them. "Fatah reminds people of their anger at losing their homes, offers them the whole loaf, of a return to all the old Palestine, predicts the Israelis will hold all the conquered territory and will have nothing to do with any of us. We offer half a loaf—half of old Palestine—and predict the Israelis will negotiate with us. The Israelis confirm not our predictions, but Fatah's. They refuse to negotiate with us, hold all the territory, refuse to budge. Why should the people not follow Fatah, with its promise of a whole loaf, instead of us, with promise of a half? What could we offer to replace that half a loaf? Only that we can actually *get* half, whereas Fatah can get nothing. But this we cannot offer, because the Israelis will not respond. It is Israel that must move if the impasse is ever to end."

I came back to talk again with the Israeli Left. Was there no hope for action on their part? Demonstrations?

Political campaigns? But they too felt despair. "The Fatah rhetoric puts us up against the wall," they said. "Let us assume Fatah means what it says now about the human beings who live in Israel being able to stay here as Jews under a unitary Palestinian state. That's not sufficient. We are not just Jewish Palestinians. There are less than a thousand Israelis who are prepared to give up having an Israeli state. Imagine if the terms the Vietnamese had set for peace had been not the withdrawal of American troops from Vietnam, but the abolition of the American state. Could you have organized Americans against the war?"

No. I could not have.

"So the Palestinians must change before we can move." Deadlock. Despair.

Only Avnery held out an inkling of hope. "Remember," he said, "what it was like in 1947. There was talk of partitioning the Mandated territory. Some of the Yishuv political parties supported this, others did not. The debate raged. One day the U.N. General Assembly voted for partition—a Jewish state, after two thousand years and the Holocaust! The BBC carried the news on radio. *Fifteen minutes later,* the whole Yishuv was in the streets—celebrating. Imagine, imagine—if Israel were to say formally, publicly, officially that we are prepared to withdraw from the West Bank and Gaza and hand over power there to Palestinians, that we will not interfere with a Palestinian uprising on the East Bank, that we will recognize a Palestinian state that includes both Banks and Gaza. Perhaps Fatah would oppose it as a sell-out of their dream of returning to Jaffa. But I think that the Palestinians would go into the streets, celebrating. . . . A state at last of their own! And the parties would soon follow them, or disappear."

When I asked him what would have to happen for an Israeli government to take such a position, he looked somehow simultaneously grim and buoyant. "Changes in Washington, changes in New York, most of all changes in Israel. We are organizing, arguing. I predict that our own party's vote will double this coming election. What more can I say? It will be hard work."

Avnery's vote did double in the fall of 1969. Since then there has been a slow and painful resurfacing of the Israeli Left; and even more slowly, it has begun to make a dent in the consciousness of Americans. But the process has been very difficult. Few Jews in America let alone non-Jewish radicals or liberals, know about Haolam Hazeh—the party Avnery leads. Few know about Siach—the group of young Socialist Zionists who utterly reject Israeli annexations of Palestinian territory, but also reject Palestinian demands for the end of the Israeli state. Few know of the existence of the Movement for Peace and Security—a kind of cross-party liberal-and-left coalition opposed to Israeli annexations of territory and urgent about the need for peace initiatives by the Israeli government. Few know about the Israeli League for Human and Civil Rights, which struggles against the Israeli military government's repression of political action by Palestinians in Gaza and the West Bank and its use on some occasions of measures like detention without trial and the destruction of houses as punishment for Palestinian activists and their friends and families.

Why this blank space? Essentially because the Jewish Establishment in the United States and the Ideological Hard Left have a tacit alliance to accomplish one result: that the only choices most Americans should hear about in the Middle East are the Meir-Dayan policy in the Israeli government, and Fatah policy (or similar policy so far as the abolition of the Israeli state is concerned) among the Palestinians.

What has been the process of this constriction of possibilities inside the Jewish community? Among the Jewish People in America a generation ago, there was a wide range of feelings toward Zionism—and if the Jewish People in the United States had been wholly free, this diversity would probably have continued in regard to the Jewish People in Israel. Some American Jews would have wanted to migrate to Israel, in accord with a belief in "return" to the land of Tanach. Some would have wanted to assist the emergence of a healthy, free, democratic, and peaceful Israel, and would at the same time have felt both free and obligated to criticize vigorously the policies or structures of Israel whenever they failed to be free, democratic, or peaceful. Some did, and would have continued to, criticize the very existence of the Israeli state, either because they believed that only in the Days of the Messiah can a true Zion living according to Jewish law be rebuilt and that anything less is a travesty, or because they felt the Diaspora was politically and spiritually a higher good than the concentration of Jews in Israel, or out of a sensitivity to the Palestinian claims to the same soil, or out of a belief that the Jewish People ought not to have a state "like other nations," or because they felt that all territorial nationalism is obsolete. It is a major oppression of the Jewish People in America that this broad range of feelings has been narrowed down almost to one or two that are allowed to be felt by any large number of Jews.

There are many ways in which this has been accomplished. In most of them, the Jewish Establishment has acted in concert with the American Empire to assert that the only "possible" choices are (1) migration to Israel, (2) total support for Israeli government policy, or (3) dropping out of the Jewish community. But it is also, sadly, true that some American radicals have responded to this repression by the Jewish Establishment by accepting these false "realities," these restricted choices permitted by the Establishment, acting as if indeed these were the only choices. They have thus been so insensitive to the legitimate range of feelings among the Jewish People as to constrict the choices available to Jewish radicals who wish to view Jewish liberation as a part of world liberation, and to many Jewish radicals this has felt like a real oppression.

Let us take up first the ways in which the Jewish Establishment, in concert with the American Empire, has tried to restrict the freedom of the Jewish People on this issue. The Empire itself has done its best to define the situation as one in which the "Cold War" against Communism is equated with protection of Israel against hostility from some Arab states and peoples, and especially from the most radical ones; in which military support for Israel is the only reasonable way of protecting or improving Israeli society and is also the only legitimate "American" position; and in which that form of support is conditioned (as in blackmail) on support of other Imperial objectives.

The Jewish Establishment has been ready—even anxious—to join in this game. It has been "more royal than the king," more militarist than the Israeli generals in defining the goals and nature of Israel. It has scorned the Israeli Left, greeted with great pleasure the constantly strengthening alliance between the Israeli government and the American Empire, supported the most capitalist elements in Israel. In twenty-five years' time it has transformed American Zionism from a movement led by labor unionists and kibbutz-oriented socialists to one dominated by wealthy businessmen. All this was to be expected from a Jewish Establishment that was itself elitist and that had during the last fifty years tied itself more and more closely to the American Empire. In accord with this policy, the Jewish Establishment has put great pressure on Jewish groups and organizations not to take anti-Imperial stands on issues of great importance in America —for example, not to oppose the Vietnam War—lest such stands endanger the Empire's commitments to the Israeli government. And the Establishment has argued that any criticism whatever of Israeli policy or social structure would weaken political support in America for the Empire's alliance with the Israeli government, and would therefore endanger Israel.

Any attempt by the Israeli Left or American Jewish Left to open up a whole new outlook—to point toward an anti-imperialist Israel at home in the Third World, protected by peace with anti-imperialist neighbors rather than by constantly escalating war against both imperialist client-states and anti-imperialists among her neighbors—any such attempt has been rigorously smashed by the American Jewish Establishment. Thus the Anti-Defamation League of B'nai B'rith pressed all Jewish organizations to avoid sponsoring, assisting, or even debating Uri Avnery when he toured America. Thus the Bundist movement—a Jewish socialist anti-Zionist movement that had great strength in the Jewish communities in Eastern Europe and America before 1940—has been systematically opposed, excluded, and where possible smashed so thoroughly that not even its history is taught to most young Jews, nor its existence mentioned.

In short, the feelings of solidarity and love—together with constant skeptical reexamination—which would have been widely felt, and legitimately so, within American Jewry toward the Jewish community in Israel, have been warped into blind hysterical support for not only the Israeli state that has been created, but for the particular policies of a particular government of that state. The responsibility for this distortion must lie upon the American Empire, the American Jewish Establishment, and the Israeli government. Its victim has been the Jewish People in America.

Indeed, the Jewish Establishment acts as if it would much rather make sure that thousands of its young people drop out of the Jewish community entirely and support Fatah's call for the dismantling of the Israeli state than encourage these young people to remain Jewish, treat Israel as a legitimate country with a disastrous foreign policy, and fight against the present Israeli Establishment and the American Jewish Establishment. As for the first way, there is nothing for the Establishment to lose: the estranged youth are not even a loss, because they are "counters" to be pointed to and deplored in Establishment maneuverings. But if the second way were taken and the youth stayed around to fight, there would be a real struggle inside the Jewish community—and the Establishment might even lose.

Meanwhile, some radical groups have asserted that the *only* legitimate position for radicals is total opposition to the existence of an Israeli state. This is indeed one legitimate position for a committed Jew to take—and some Jews who were fully committed to the Jewish People have, for a number of reasons suggested above, taken that position for centuries past. But it is not the *only* legitimate position for radical Jews who are committed to the liberation of the world and the Jewish People. Attempts to insist on it as the only legitimate position stem from one of two mistakes in radical or revolutionary feeling or analysis:

Either, in regard to the situation in America, from lack of understanding of or hostility to the very notion of a Jewish People in America which would have some special concerns for the Jewish People elsewhere;

Or, in regard to the situation in the Middle East, from an understandable but shortsighted rejection of the deep dilemmas created there by the real emergence, during the past generation, of an Israeli people which is entitled to self-determination and which must at the same time deal justly with a Palestinian people that is also entitled to self-determination.

What is worse, some elements of what might be called the Hard Left seem to believe it is politically much more rewarding to demand, from young Jewish radicals particularly, a total commitment to an anti-Israel line than to explore the grays and greens and purples of a recognition that there are both an Israeli and a Palestinian people, and that neither is entitled to oppress or destroy the other. Much better to shatter the lingering emotional connections of young Jews to Israel than to encourage the creation of radicalism out of the acceptance and the refinement of one's own deepest emotional identities, if one is indeed trying to build a Hard Left rather than a New Left.

And on both sides, Zionist and Hard Left, it is easier to appeal to the American *machismo* of rifles and jets than to encourage the gentler compassions for two peoples caught in fear of each other and longing for the same territory.

The dangers of this blind assumption that there are no choices other than Fatah and Meir-Dayan became most sharply clear in September 1970, when the Palestinian uprising in Jordan was faced with the threat of a jointly planned Israeli-American action to uphold the power of King Hussein. During that month thousands of Palestinians were massacred by a "Jordanian" army overwhelmingly paid for by American money, using American tanks and mortars. The crisis began because some of the Palestinian nationalists felt that the proposed Rogers Plan for peace in the Middle East was nicely calculated to appeal to Soviet, Egyptian, Jordanian, Israeli, and American interests—but also calculated to be "the permanent solution" of the Palestinian problem: permanently subjecting the Palestinians to Jordanian and Israeli control. They acted in desperation—and as some of their comrades felt, unwisely—to shatter the Rogers Plan through the airplane hijackings. The result was the upheaval inside Jordan.

It seems that the United States made clear to the Soviet Union that there would be an American-protected Israeli intervention in Jordan if Syrian tanks were not withdrawn. The Soviet Union (which has no special love for the Palestinians anyway) then insisted to Syria that its tanks be removed, and the Syrians agreed. Thus the Palestinians were defeated and Hussein protected. This was a defeat for the long-run interests of the Israeli people—which would have been best served by a Palestinian victory and the emergence of a Palestinian government with which Israel could have negotiated a just peace on the basis of both Israeli and Palestinian self-determination.

But let us examine what would have been the result had the threats not worked, and an American-backed Israeli intervention actually occurred.

The Palestinians would have been brought to the brink of a genocidal disaster. But it was not only the Palestinians who would have been deeply damaged, if the United States and Israel had sent planes and guns roaring into Jordan. So would all the other decent interests in the struggle; only the large special business, military, and political interests would have benefited and even they probably only in the short run—just as they benefited only in the short run from the Vietnam War.

Let us run down the list:

The Palestinians would have been decimated or worse. In the long run, this might have helped stoke Arab revolutionary feeling against the Arab governments; in the short run, it would have strengthened those governments: King Hussein, the Saudi monarchy, probably even the Egyptian government.

Israel would have found itself first trying to justify the unjustifiable. The government's official position was that any intervention would be aimed not at the Palestinians but at Syrian tanks which might pose at some later date a threat to Israel. But on that theory, any conceivable "preventive" strike against a hostile state's military forces is "defensive" no matter how long away the danger is. Israel was militarily dominant in September 1970, the Arab alliance was weaker than ever. Israel had a stronger ally than ever. Threats of a "preventive" strike were obviously a cover for the *result*—regardless of intention—that Hussein would be protected against the Palestinians.

Then, when Israel had consolidated its occupation of most of Jordan, it would have begun trying to govern even more Palestinians. Either it would have killed or expelled scores or hundreds of thousands, destroying its own soul once and for all, permanently blackening its name among liberals and radicals throughout the world, and

fueling an undying hatred from the whole Arab world—
which had recently begun to unravel its hostility—or it
would have tried to keep governing the angriest, most
dedicated Palestinians of all. The latter course would have
meant the swift erosion of liberty and justice in Israel.

The United States would almost certainly have been
polarized along these lines: the Pentagon, Nixon-Agnew-
Mitchell, and almost the entire "organized Jewish community" (i.e., the official Jewish leadership) supporting
an American military intervention; almost all of Middle
America, non-Jewish liberal America, Black America, and
radical America opposed. To many it would have seemed
that American boys were being sent by the Jews and the
Pentagon to die for an Israel that was not even in serious
danger. The danger of an anti-Semitic blacklash would
have been great—and what allies would the Jewish people have had? The Pentagon, and the Nixon-Agnew-Mit-
chell machine! The worst allies conceivable; in the long
run, those allies most exposed to popular wrath. It would
have been like having the Tsar, and only the Tsar, on our
side in 1904.

Jews—Israeli or American—who were planning to
bring about a Israeli-American intervention to save King
Hussein were not only betraying their own belief in the
Judaism of the Prophets and its partial modern transla-
tion into democracy, national self-determination, or socialism, but were also endangering the future liberties of the
Israeli nation and the Jewish People.

It should be accepted as the task of non-Establishment
Jews of every ideological persuasion—left Zionist, liberal
secular, religious, pacifist, Yiddishist, socialist—to prevent
these dangers of an American-Israeli intervention in any
Arab state against an Arab revolutionary movement, and
to organize against any Jewish Establishment that is so
careless of the future of the Jewish People. Even Jews
who believe in an American intervention to protect Israel
itself, and who would be prepared to accept the dangers

of such a course, should be prepared to oppose an American intervention on behalf of the Arab Establishments against their own people.

But more basically and more permanently, American Jews who have a feeling of special commitment to Israel or to "Zion," the seriously Jewish communities inside Israel, have another task: to make clear in the Jewish and general American communities that the choice of policy is *not* between the Meir-Dayan government and Fatah policy. It is our task to analyze and organize: to explain publicly that there is an Israeli people which is entitled to self-determination, and that within Israel there is a serious debate over Israeli policy. That on the one hand there are some Israelis who want to keep the West Bank permanently for military reasons, some ultra-Orthodox religious groups that want to hold it for "religious" reasons, some business interests that want to exploit the labor and markets of the occupied territories and the raw materials of Sinai, some super-patriots who simply want to extend Israel's land area. Together, these forces seek to paralyze any movement for a satisfactory political solution to the Palestinian problem. And so long as Israelis are forced to keep on being military governors, the more right wing the country will become. Thus Arab poets are jailed and Arab houses blown up as reprisals for guerrilla action—not just the houses of the guerrillas, but others merely suspect of being their associates. And Israelis, too, are beginning to suffer as the country becomes more polarized: Israelis who participate in demonstrations against their government's policies, even when like Siach they make clear their commitment to Zionism, are condemned by the press and beaten by the police.

But we must make clear that there are Israelis who oppose and resist these policies. And we should ourselves reach out to Israelis who oppose religious bigotry and conformism, support vigorously the kibbutz and other new socialist and democratic processes, and ally themselves to the Third World—e.g., to Vietnamese victims of America rather than America the aggressor. Such groups as Haolam Hazeh, the Movement for Peace and Security, Siach—all of which look toward the preservation of Israeli society on a new basis—and even Matzpen, which seeks to persuade Israelis to choose voluntarily the dissolution of the Israeli state—must be much better known and understood to Americans—Jewish and non-Jewish, radical and nonradical. Even though we may disagree with some of their policies, committed Jews should arrange for them to come to the United States as speakers, make their publications available, etc.

But even this is not all. Radical Jews have an obligation to speak honestly and clearly to the Palestinian nationalist movements and their supporters in the American radical movement. As Jews, above all, we must tell the Palestinians that we in some sense understand and share their anguish at what they have lost and at what they suffer. Who, after all, should better understand the pain of those who feel cut off from the Dome of the Rock on the Temple Mount than we, who were deprived of the Temple? And if some Jews—most Jews—do not understand their pain, we are all the more obligated to do so. We must be clear that even when we disagree with them, we do so with a full sense of how hard their situation is, and with a radically human outreach to their need.

We must tell them that we believe it is not revolutionary to deny self-determination to any people, and that there is an Israeli people.

We must tell them that we recognize and honor the changes they have wrought in Palestinian consciousness during the last five years—bringing it from hostility toward the bare existence of Israelis in Palestine to the acceptance of the permanent residence of the human beings who live in Israel, and bringing it from support for all the most reactionary nationalist Arab governments to hostility against the right-wing Arab states. We must say that we hope this double process will continue—to become more radical vis-à-vis the Arab Establishment and more open vis-à-vis the legitimacy of the Israeli people.

We must tell them that we believe radical changes in Israeli society can never come if they are flinging all Israelis up against the wall; that only after a period of peace and self-confidence and the removal of fear will Israelis be able to move toward social transformation at home, and be able even to imagine the creation of a broader Middle Eastern political body of some sort, or the construction of the kind of bi-national state that such Zionists as Martin Buber and Mapam used to dream of.

We must tell them that we believe violence is the last resort, not the first resort, of revolutionaries—and that even the Vietnamese explored the possibilities of nonviolence before they took up guns. We must say that we believe the revolutionary goals of human freedom and justice might be far better shown in action and reality in the Middle East by Palestinians who were prepared to use militant demonstrations, walk-ins, strikes—deeds of life—than by guerrilla bombings and hijackings—deeds of death. But we must also be honest enough to say that we do not know whether we ourselves would be able to respond solely with nonviolence to a military occupation or to the kind of massacre that Hussein visited upon the Palestinians.

We must say that we are already organizing in the Jewish community a dedicated opposition to the oppressive elements of Israeli policy; and that we hope they will do the same among Palestinians, to change the anti-human elements of the policies of some of the Palestinian organizations. And that we expect them to share with us, and with the Israeli Left, not a desire to destroy our different peoples and traditions and identities, but a desire to honor those differences in freedom and in equality.

As we say these things to the Palestinians and their supporters, we must be clear to ourselves that we would have no right to say them if we did not feel ourselves to be their sisters and brothers—sisters and brothers because they, however mistaken, are struggling to free their people as we are struggling to free ours.

I believe that in these ways we who are radical Jews in America would be most deeply honoring and aiding that which is Zion within Israel.

Avodah Bet

I—My Vine, My Figtree:
An Article by Sharon Rose
Published in Win *Magazine, June 15, 1970*

Once, in another life (nice Jewish girl from New York, just graduated from college, about to launch brilliant career as mathematician—computer expert) I travelled to Israel. I stayed on a Kibbutz and picked grapes and peaches and dug the whole scene: the communal dining hall and children's houses; the pioneer-farmers, rifles at their sides, who had unearthed enough prehistoric artifacts to fill their own small museum. Using the Bible as a guide book, I reached out to touch the walls on either side of a narrow street in Nazareth—a street that hasn't changed much—except for the Coca Cola stand—since Jesus walked down it. Riding a bus in Haifa on the Sabbath I learned how the Labor Movement is powerful enough in that city to defeat the ultra-Orthodox who keep public facilities in the rest of the country shut down on that day. Wandering in the Mea Shearim quarter of Jerusalem, I tried to comprehend in what sense the strange people there, in their long black costumes, are kin to me. I disdained the American tourists who complained of the service at the posh Tel Aviv (read Miami Beach) hotels, and joined them, weeping, at the Anne Frank memorial to the six million.

I did see things that troubled my liberal head. I stood on the shore at Elath, looked across the Gulf to its twin city, Jordanian Acaba, and bemoaned the wasted duplication, the millions spent on armaments to keep two economies separated: two economies where there should be one. And I asked embarrassing questions: Why are all the dock workers and other laborers dark skinned Moroccan Jews and Arabs? Why are all the ditch diggers and workers on the roads dark skinned Yemenite Jews and Arabs? Why do the "Socialist" Kibbutzim join in the exploitation of this labor? Why do the Arab villages live under military rule? Why are crucial civil rights denied Palestinian Arabs who remained in Israel? My Mapamnik (Left wing, Socialist Zionist) friends had high-minded answers: "It's just that the oriental Jews have not yet acquired the skills of our technological (read Western) economy. As soon as they do they will be integrated, or their children will be. After all, we cannot allow our country to be Levantine." "It's just that peace has not come yet. As soon as it does the Israeli Arabs will become full citizens."

And I answered: "But you are Levantine, or you should be. It is you who should be integrated: into the Middle East."

So I saw that I am not a Zionist, and I came home to my brilliant career. The day I arrived was the day Martin Luther King led his march on Washington. And I said, "Right—the struggle for civil rights is the same wherever it is fought!"

Now, in this life, I know that liberation is not achieved by finding optimal solutions to neat equations. If a system requires a pool of cheap labor to exploit, it will not be changed by asking the exploiters for part of the pie. If I was not a Zionist then, I am certainly not one now. For me, my own liberation, and liberation for all the Jewish people is inexorably tied to liberation for all peoples. My life is dedicated to organizing for that liberation through revolutionary change. Fully recognizing the dialectic that exists between Marxism and my cultural nationalism, I choose to organize in the community I think I can still talk to best: the Jewish community.

I say I believe that we can talk best to the Jewish community, but I admit it is becoming more difficult to do so all the time. One reason is that the Jewish community is becoming harder and harder to find. If a "community" is a set of people with common cultural experiences, supportive of common needs and interests, perhaps we should not so designate American Jewry, perhaps we should call it instead, the "Jewish rung" on the economic ladder that is the Amerikan system. And where is the Jewish rung? In suburbia, of course (or at least, on the suburban fringes of large cities) where all "good" white people who consent to be melted down in the Amerikan melting pot are eventually sent to reap the dubious "rewards" of having undertaken the climb up the ladder in the first place.

So off we go to suburbia, to the Jewish communal places, such as they are, to talk about how, as long as the ladder exists, those who oppress the people on the rungs below them will be equally oppressed by those on the rungs above them; about how it is that the Jews of Amerika remain a marginal people, as do all ethnic minorities; about how it is the responsibility of the Jewish community to help Jewish merchants get out of Black ghettoes, and to see to it that there are no Jewish slumlords and segregationists; about why so many Jewish young people are rejecting a brand of religion that is irrelevant to the real struggles of our time, and what the community might do about it. And a dialogue of sorts, strained and tenuous as it may be, is established, until the inevitable moment when someone in the room asks: "And what is your position on Israel?"

Now that question is a trap, because the person who asks it recognizes only two possible positions: the position he or she attributes (equally) to El Fatah and all the Arab states (namely, that "All the Jews of Israel will be pushed into the sea"), and the position he or she views as the only "Jewish" position (namely, the rigid, militaristic, morally and tactically indefensible stance of the present Israeli regime).

We must not fall into that trap, for the very inevitability of that question and the fact that it admits of only two responses lies at the heart of what is wrong with our system. A rich cultural heritage based on a prophetic religious tradition has been largely forfeited to the Amerikan melting pot, to be replaced by an uneasy, guilt-ridden quasi-loyalty to a foreign state. It is a bind loyalty—one which forces Amerikan "Zionists" into the absurd positions of favoring disestablishmentarian religious liberty here, while defending the existence of a theocracy in the Middle East, of attesting to the survival of the Jewish people through two millennia of "dispersion" from their homeland, while denying the existence of a Palestinian people after their twenty-five years or less as refugees.

From what does that uncritical loyalty of "Zionists" in Amerika stem? I put the word in quotes to indicate that the people to whom I refer actually have no serious desire or intention to emigrate to Israel. When pushed, most of the same people admit that their "Zionism" is based on a real fear that Amerika could produce another wave of anti-Semitism from which they could take refuge in the Jewish state. That this fear is real, however, is no reason to allow it to go unchallenged. For the "refuge" theory is a dangerous self-delusion. The Amerikan system does show every sign of becoming expert at genocide. Unless we stop it now, there will be no piece of real estate far enough away, no cave deep enough in the earth to protect any of us. My organizing to help stop that genocide requires that I ally myself with brothers and sisters in the black community who are organizing to prevent a race war here, and against whom the repression has already begun to be unleashed. I think they are dead wrong whenever they attempt to use anti-Semitism to increase the class consciousness of their own people, but I will not

allow even that to put me in the position of defending un-
equivocally the foreign policy of any government.

The question is not whether the state of Israel has a
right to exist. People have rights—states only responsibilities. Whatever might have been my position on the partition of Palestine in 1948 (and I do not agree that Israel
was created "to serve as a lacky of Western imperialism,"
but rather, I view the Palestinians, Jews and Arabs as
victims of the clash between imperialist expansion from
the East and West), it seems clear now that the state of
Israel has not met its responsibilities towards its own people and towards finding a response to the legitimate demands of self determination of the Palestinian Arabs.

The revolution will come to Israel. There are indications that some left wing Israelis have learned that they
must help build it. The Palestinian Arabs will gain self
determination, despite the best efforts of the present regimes of the Arab states and their Amerikan oil company
supporters. I believe that a bi-national, democratic, secular state, encompassing the entire area of the original
mandate, will provide the best environment to carry out
such revolutions, to create a truly just economic system
for all the peoples of the area. If I were a Zionist, I
would be there, working for that.

That is my "position" on the Middle East. But we are
here, and we have a country to turn around, before it
destroys the entire world, the Middle East included.
Sometime soon, I hope, we will begin seriously to discuss
our own oppression and liberation—liberation from a system which has forced us to relinquish our heritage. Where
should that liberation begin? Why, with the very ground
we stand on. It will be necessary to liberate the synagogues (and, by the way, the churches, which, I think,
have become equally irrelevant to the Christianity they
were built to serve) from the power-worshipping Amerikan anti-religion they foster. We will breathe new life
and meaning into our traditions. For we understand that

it is better to be Jewish, Catholic, Irish, Buddhist, Italian, Black, Spanish, Puerto Rican . . . anything but melted down, homogenized, assimilated, and dead, Amerikan. Then "all peoples will walk every one in the name of his god, and we will walk in the name of the Lord our God for ever and ever." (Micah, 4:4)

II—Memorandum of the Anti-Defamation League of B'nai B'rith

TO:	ADL Regional Offices	NOT FOR PUB-LICATION
FROM:	Abraham H. Foxman	FOR YOUR BACK-GROUND IN-FORMATION ONLY
DATE:	September 18, 1970	
SUBJECT:	Uri Avnery	

The Fellowship of Reconciliation, a pacifist group which has spawned the Catholic Peace Fellowship and the Jewish Peace Fellowship, in conjunction with the American Friends Service Committee is sponsoring a nationwide tour of Uri Avnery, a member of the Israeli Knesset, to speak on the Middle East crisis. Avnery arrived in the United States last week, has already met in Washington with several senators and representatives of the State Department and plans to travel throughout the country to address college groups and civic organizations.

As an opponent of the traditional concepts of Zionism and Judaism, Avnery may say things which will trouble and even embarrass the Jewish community. Attached you will find a fact sheet outlining his views prepared by our Research and Evaluation Department.

In normal times, Avnery's views, which reflect the

thinking of a small minority in Israel, would be of no special concern to us; however, Avnery's public appearances in the United States, coming at a time when Arab and pro-Arab propagandists have adopted several of his concepts, specifically his use of the term "de-Zionization" —long an Arab euphemism for the destruction of the Jewish state—could aid the Arab cause. The enemies of Israel will surely exploit his presence to project some of his concepts in the United States, specifically his views on world Zionism and "de-Zionization."

Avnery is not in the mainstream of Israel's political life. But as Israel is a democracy, he is free to express his minority view not only in the Israeli parliament but through his publication and on public platforms.

We advise that Jewish organizations not sponsor or co-sponsor his appearances and not engage in public debate with him.

Outlined briefly below (in addition to the more detailed fact sheet attached) are some of the concepts which Avnery has in the past projected which we believe you should be aware of:

—He advocates the abolition of Zionist ideology in Israel, its institutions and traditional Jewish aspirations.

—He is against any incorporation or annexation of the administered territory and is against the establishment of Jewish settlements in administered areas until peace is achieved.

—He advocates that all Arab refugees be given the choice between repatriation or compensation.

On the other hand, although several of Avnery's attitudes may add fuel to Arab propaganda, you should be aware of some positive points in his program:

—He has spoken out against a bi-national state advocated by Arab terrorist groups and the new Left and has called for the creation of a separate Arab Republic of Palestine outside of Israel.

—He has stated that Israel should exist as a sovereign

state which should be open to "all people" of the Middle East and specifically as a haven for Jewish immigrants.

—He is violently opposed to Al Fatah and terrorist activities believing them to be detrimental to the speedy achievement of peace.

—He has spoken out against Arab extremists.

—He opposes any Israeli withdrawal from territories before peace is established.

—He strongly opposes Matzpen and its spokesmen. Avnery criticized Matzpen and Aryeh Bober in an editorial he wrote for the July 29, 1970 issue of his publication *Haolam Hazeh:*

"I do not know many young men who arouse in me rejection and repulsion as the young man called Aryeh Bober. . . .

"He and 30 other members of Matzpen tried to establish in the Haolam Hazeh party underground cells in order to dismember it from within. . . .

"All the heads of this group sit abroad, where they publish blasphemies against the state in a peculiar anti-Semitic shade. . . ."

Speaking about the Committee of New Alternatives in the Middle East headed by Noam Chomsky which sponsored Bober's speaking tour in the U.S., Avnery wrote:

". . . an efficient mysterious organization in the United States obtained for him (Bober) signatures of important naive personalities, arranged for his lectures at important universities, brought him on TV screens and organized for him meetings to raise funds."

The following is his tentative itinerary. Please keep us informed.

September 15   Arrive in United States

        16   Institute for Policy Studies—Washington, D.C.

        17   American Friends Service Committee—Washington, D.C.

19	Johns Hopkins University—Baltimore, Md.
21	Brandeis University—Boston, Mass.
22	Georgetown University—Washington, D.C.
23	Boston University and M.I.T.—Boston & Cambridge, Mass.
24-25	Harvard University—Cambridge, Mass.
28	Amherst, Smith & Springfield Colleges—Amherst, Northhampton and Springfield, Mass.
29	University of Connecticut—Storrs, Conn.
30	Press Conference—Boston, Mass.
October 2-3	Middle East Institute Conference—Washington, D.C.
4-5	Yale University—New Haven, Conn.
6	Wesleyan University—Middletown, Conn.
7	University of California—Los Angeles, Calif.
8	University of Chicago—Chicago, Ill.
12	Columbia University—New York City
13	New York University—New York City
14	Princeton University—Princeton, N.J.
16	University of Toronto—Toronto, Canada
17	Return to Israel

The various Jewish student campus groups, including the Israeli Student Association, are aware of his itinerary and are familiar with his ideology and will challenge him whenever necessary.

AHF: gh
Attach
cc: Community Relations Councils
Middle Eastern Affairs Committee

(There followed a three-page single-spaced detailed dossier on Avnery's life and politics.)

*III—For Peace and Justice in the Middle East:
A Position Paper of Jews for Urban Justice
Adopted November 10, 1970*

1. *Self-determination for the Palestinian people.*
   We urge the government of Israel to state publicly at once that it recognizes that there is a Palestinian people living on the East and West Banks of Jordan and in Gaza; that it believes the whole Palestinian people is entitled to national self-determination and full independence in those areas; that it is prepared to enter negotiations with the whole range of Palestinian leadership, including but not limited to the P.L.O., over the best means of achieving the desirable end of Palestinian national self-determination and full independence; and that it will bend all its diplomatic and political efforts to achieving that end despite opposition by any other government.

2. *Self-determination for the Israeli people.*
   We urge the leadership of the Palestinian people, including the P.L.O., to do the same by stating publicly at once that they recognize that there is an Israeli people which is entitled to national self-determination and full independence within its own boundaries; and that it is prepared to enter negotiations with the Israeli government on the best means of achieving Palestinian self-determination and independence. We urge the leadership of other Arab peoples to state publicly, at once, that they recognize that there is an Israeli people which is entitled to national self-determination and full independence within its own boundaries.

3. *No Israeli intervention in Arab struggles.*
   We urge the Israeli government to state publicly at once that it will not intervene militarily in any civil

war in any Arab country, nor in any war between Arab peoples, and that it would welcome the end of the rule of repressive governments in Jordan and other Arab states if the people living there so will it.

4. *No U.S. or Soviet intervention in Arab struggles.*

We vigorously oppose any military intervention by the United States or Soviet governments in any civil war within any Arab country or in any war between Arab peoples; and we urge the United States and Soviet governments to state publicly that they would welcome the end of the rule of repressive governments in Jordan and other Arab states if the people living there so will it.

5. *We are opposed to all acts of genocide.*

We are opposed to genocide whether it be in the forms of cultural, physical, or psychological oppression. This principle must be applied to all peoples in the Middle East whether or not they are a minority or a majority in any existing or proposed political unit.

IV—The Liberation of Palestine and Israel
Statement published in the
New York Review, *July 1, 1971*

All the peoples of the Middle East are entitled to liberation—liberation from war, from the Imperial designs of the great powers, from exploitation of their labor and resources, from oppression by neighboring peoples or oligarchic governments, from genocide. Liberation to determine their own destinies.

All the peoples. Including Palestinians. Including Israelis.

Today both Israeli and Palestinian political leaders refuse to recognize the legitimate right of the other side to exist as a people. Each side appeals to "history" to prove that the other side never existed or never should have existed.

But history is less important to human justice than is present human reality. Whatever should have happened in the Middle East two thousand years ago, two hundred years ago, twenty years ago, or two years ago, now both an Israeli people and a Palestinian people do exist.

Israel cannot make a just peace with the governments of Jordan or Egypt or Syria or the Soviet Union, while she ignores the Palestinians. And the Palestinians cannot simply treat Israel as an extension of Western imperialism, for although the Israeli government *has* allied itself with the Western Empires, an Israeli people exists and they will not disappear, except through genocide.

It is not "revolutionary" to force a people to abandon self-determination. Indeed, that demand posed to Israel is precisely what freezes the Israeli Left and prevents it from creating the socialist reconstruction of Israel which many Palestinians say they hope for. And the Israeli government's insistence on dealing with the Jordanian monarchy, rather than with Palestinian nationalists on the East or West Banks, helps that monarchy—a client of the American Empire, and the most direct and most nakedly violent oppressor of the Palestinians—to prevent the Palestinian people from taking into their own hands the building of a decent society—as many Israelis say they hope will happen.

And if—as some Palestinians and some Israelis say— the hope is someday to reunite in some form the areas where Israelis and Palestinians now live, without destroying either people, peace is required so that both peoples may make free choices.

But present policies on both sides do not lead to peace or liberation. Instead, they lead to paranoia, internal repression, increasing military confrontation, and ultimately to genocide of one or both peoples.

We cannot shrug off these prospects. We have a stake in the survival and the full liberation of the Israeli people.

We have an equal stake in the survival and full liberation of the Palestinian people. And we have a stake in preventing the U.S. government and American corporations from pursuing business-imperial adventures in the Middle East: no matter which "side" they seem to support, the rulers of America pursue as their overriding aim the maximizing of their own power and profits in the Middle East, and use any power and profits they win there to increase their power over us.

Only if popular pressures for peace and social justice increase among both the Israeli and Palestinian peoples can peace between them be made possible. But the first steps toward change must come from the militarily more powerful partner. Today Israel occupies a great part of the territory in which Palestinians live; no Israelis live under alien rule. *Therefore, we call on Israel to announce at once that she accepts the full right of the Palestinian people to a state of their own where they now live, including the East and West Banks and Gaza, that she is prepared to negotiate with the whole range of Palestinian leadership on how to withdraw Israeli troops from the West Bank and Gaza, and that she will not intervene in Jordan against any effort by the Palestinian majority there to topple the monarch so as to reunite East and West Banks under Palestinian rule.*

Once Israel cuts the Gordian knot, Palestinians must respond. (Until then, any Palestinians who reach out may be seen as Uncle Toms by their people.) *We urge that if Israel makes the commitment to a free Palestine, the Palestine Liberation Organization and other Palestinian leaders proclaim their readiness to accept the right of Israelis to self-determination, to discuss with Israel the process of how to withdraw Israeli troops, and to negotiate a peace with Israel once all Israeli troops have withdrawn.*

Finally, we urge Americans to expose and organize against the Imperial adventures of their own governments and huge corporations in the Middle East. We urge that the de facto collaboration of United States and Soviet military services in encouraging a Middle East arms race also be exposed and ended. We urge resistance to any U.S. intervention in Jordan to support the Jordanian monarchy against the Palestinian majority. We urge that the American Jewish community and the American anti-war and radical movements take up these issues—not by a mindless endorsement of one party orthodoxy or another in the Middle East, but with serious study and a sensitive commitment to the liberation of both the Israeli and the Palestinian people from militarism and exploitation.

Barbara Bick	Stewart Meacham
Noam Chomsky	Anatol Rapoport
Douglas Dowd	Alan Rinzler
David Gelber	Leonard Rodberg
Todd Gitlin	Sharon Rose
Mitchell Goodman	John Ruskay
Rabbi Arthur Green	Paul Schifman
Abbie Hoffman	Rabbi Robert Siegel
Paul Jacobs	Benjamin Spock
Louis Kampf	Mike Tabor
Sidney Lens	Kenneth Tilsen
Michael Lerner	Arthur Waskow
Denise Levertov	Rabbi Arnold Jacob Wolf
Michael Maccoby	Robert Zevin

*The Crisis
of American Jewry*

III

The Crisis of American Jewry

To understand the changes going on inside myself, to understand the growing radical Jewish movement that I felt increasingly a part of, and to understand the kind of opposition that we faced from within and without the Jewish community, I found it more and more important to see ourselves as individual examples of a social event: the crisis of American Jewry. That crisis is really a triple crisis, occurring at three different levels of intensity. The first is what might be called an eighty-year crisis, the problem faced by the Jewish community in the United States as its eighty-year-long career of assimilation into being "American" came to an end. The second is a nineteen-hundred-year problem, in the sense that the American Diaspora—and other Diaspora communities as well —have to cope for the first time since the destruction of the Temple with the issue of their own meaning and value as part of the Jewish People, now that there is a state of Israel. And finally there is what might be called the thirty-five-hundred-year crisis: what is the meaning and value of the whole Jewish experience since Sinai, facing the era of the Holocaust and Hiroshima, facing the era in which the destruction of the human race is possible?

Let us begin with the eighty-year crisis. To help us understand it, here is a thumbnail history of the Jewish community in America:

In the 1890s, the mass migration of Jews from Eastern Europe created for the first time a large Jewish community in the United States. It was indeed a "community": integral, unalienated. In it elements that are now usually known separately as "religion," "politics," "culture," "ethics," "economics," "the family," were felt, experienced, and lived through as a seamless whole. "Halacha"—the code of behavior—was not an externalized system of law but a Path, a Way, in which the community lived, integrating ideas and action.

The community was deeply poor, so thoroughly "un-American" in dress, politics, even smell, as to horrify those who ruled America and even those Jews who had come earlier in much smaller numbers and had rather easily become assimilated. Often it was socialist, and bitterly angry about the naked economic oppression it suffered from the American system.

The community was, however, grateful to discover that the legal disabilities placed upon being a Jew were far less onerous than in Europe. The laws made citizenship available on equal terms to Jews as individuals, while denying the possibility of the *community's* having some kind of legally recognized role in American society. The political, economic, and educational structures of America rewarded the learning of English and the abandonment of Yiddish, and the public schools did their best to ignore and uproot Jewish culture and to reward "Americanization." The celebration of the Shabbat in any profound way as a day of tranquillity, contemplation, study, and joy was made extremely difficult—and the price in economic and political terms made high for those who insisted on pursuing the Shabbat. The other Holy Days were stripped of their moral and political meaning and some, such as Chanukah, which began as a radical celebration of a national liberation struggle, were commercialized. The rabbi (a people's teacher and life-long student) was turned into an institutional clergyman. A calendar built around the fusion of humanity into the world of nature was reduced to insignificance in order to fit the business needs of industrial capitalism. The process of *Torah lishma,* studying Torah for its own sake, and even the secularization of this impulse in the study of art and science for their own sake, was broken by the capitalist ethic, seeking technological advance or social pacification. The traditionally male role as student of Torah was translated into "Making It," the female conflict-resolution role cheapened into manipulation of the family. Thus was created the desanctified family-competition scene typified by the Super-Bar Mitzvah.

Meanwhile, drawing on the special skills (in literacy, urban life, and business training) of the Jewish migrants, the American system began to slot the angry Jewish poor of the great Eastern cities into a particular economic role: that of the middleman between the great institutions of commercial and industrial power, and the industrial working class and under-class. Much greater proportions of the Jewish community than of other migrant groups of the same period, and overwhelmingly greater proportions than of such later arrivals en masse in the city as Blacks and Puerto Ricans, were channeled into the more comfortable life of the middle class. From about 1925 on, Jews found themselves first the grocers, rent collectors, landlords, and moneylenders of the poor, and then in the next generation—from about 1950 on—increasingly the teachers, social workers, and physicians of the poor. The political bent of the Jewish community shifted from radical to liberal. Meanwhile, confronted first with the Holocaust and then with the creation and difficulties of the state of Israel, American Jews reorganized themselves separately from other Americans. But this separateness was not an organic expression of differences between their own life process and that of other Americans; such differences were more and more disappearing. Instead the new organizational forms grew out of a much more "alienated," "policy" concern: the protection of Jewish communities abroad. At the same time Jews were becoming more and more "American" in their daily lives, they were becoming more and more what they called "Zionist" —Israel-centered—in their heads. By 1965 almost all organized non-Zionist or anti-Zionist Judaism had disappeared.

Thus from 1890 to 1965, two major changes had taken

place in the life of the Jewish People in the United States —a change in communal form, and a change in economic status and function. Both were complex mixtures of good and evil. Legal equality for Jews was accompanied by the partial dissolution of the organic Jewish community, and its replacement by a network of organization focused elsewhere. Economic advances for Jews were accompanied by the slotting of Jews into the role of "mini-oppressor" in the larger society—a classic role of classic dangers for Jews in Western society. But until 1965, most American Jews focused not on what they had given up or been reduced to, but upon the benefits they had received.

From 1965 to 1970, a succession of events plunged into crisis this whole process of increasing upward-mobile self-confidence as Americans. First came the mid-'60s crisis of the Black movement and the Black community. From the 1940s until 1964, the major thrust of Black energy had been to undermine Southern White power and to join the American melting pot. Most Jews had been willing to support that effort; some Jews went South to join it, or stayed North to organize real assistance. But in 1964 it became clear that Black inclusion raised the temperature of the melting pot too high. The place and moment at which the pot cracked can be pinpointed to Atlantic City, when the liberal political party of the United States said it had no way of replacing racist plantation owners with Black sharecroppers as the recognized Democrats of Mississippi. From that moment on, the thrust of Black energies shifted from integration to "Black Power." And from that moment on, the melting pot began to disintegrate. First the Blacks, then Chicanos and Puerto Ricans and Indians, then Jews and Appalachians, and a little more slowly Italians and Poles began to reject the melting pot—or simply to discover that it was not there.

Simultaneously, the Vietnam War shaped the consciousness of a whole generation of American youth—and often shaped it into not wanting to be "American." To young Jews especially, the war was an earthquake. Brought up on memories of the Holocaust and genocide, they were horrified to discover that the United States government—which they had been taught defended the world against Hitler—was behaving in Vietnam like Hitler. "Genocide," "Holocaust," began to ring with new meaning among these young Jews. They linked the Nazis to the present by naming their government "Amerika." They, whose parents had proudly embraced the American Promise, the quasi-Methodist suburban synagogue, and the quasi-Rotarian B'nai B'rith lodge, fiercely rejected being Americans at all. Some chose to become "Indians" or members of the "Woodstock Nation." Others became Jews.

Finally, the third element in this disconnection from America: the Middle East war of June 1967. For two weeks before the war broke out in open violence, it looked to most Jews in America as if Israel were in mortal danger, and as if the United States government did not care and would not help. At that existential moment, most Jews discovered a gut attachment to Israel that was so deep that they surprised themselves with an outpouring of energy that seemed utterly different from the puzzlement and doubts of non-Jewish America—and with an upwelling of anger against the United States government. That anger was controlled, swallowed, channeled; but it was there. Israel's military triumph in the war and the next few years of permanent tension in the Middle East created new kinds of strains, but practically all Jews —those who totally supported Israel's actions, and also Jews who were critical of Israeli policy and even Jews who became critical of Israel's existence—discovered they were far more deeply, more emotionally involved in the Middle East than they were in dealing with other conflicts round the globe. They felt about Israel as they felt about America: somehow, they were responsible for its existence *and/or* for its injustices. Simply because they were Jewish.

Thus from 1965 to 1970 the eighty-year-long upward-mobile process—up and into America—was shattered. To many it became not simply impracticable, as during periodic economic slumps, but undesirable—a much more basic crisis in belief. So many of the Jewish youth began to celebrate, not mourn, the end of the melting pot—and to herald the re-creation of a real Jewish community. They began to talk about the creation of newly Halachic communities—not accepting blindly the code of behavior set forth in the traditional Halacha, but accepting the basic premise of the seamless life process that unites ideas and action, and does it "Jewishly." They began to criticize as assimilationists those Establishment elders who had triumphed in the triumphs of America.

But they did not take the whole of American Jewry with them. Most Jews have not quite understood the crisis, even though they are shaken by its intensity. And most of the Establishment Jews of the 1940s and 1950s have responded to the disintegration of "America" not with celebration but with panic, and to criticism from the young not with change but with fury.

This last development requires exploration. It is easy enough to say that of course the elders are still wedded to what they still think was their own success in joining America. But they have not simply stayed where they were; during the period of crisis they have moved swiftly toward much greater dependence on the rulers of America, have stopped defining themselves even as liberals, and have replaced their own previous tolerance of radicals with furious attacks upon the radicals. What is more, not just the thin layer of the Jewish Establishment but sizable numbers of the middle class and the Jewish poor have moved in the same direction—have created the Jewish Defense League as the clearest expression of this new rightward trend, have moved almost every formerly liberal Jewish organization to the right.

"To the right" in two senses: both in the direction of a more status quo-oriented social policy, and toward a far more constricted discussion of possibilities within the Jewish community.

For example, in 1969 B'nai B'rith called together about twenty-five "intellectuals" in their Washington headquarters, under the chairmanship of former White House assistant Myer Feldman, to talk about the situation of American Jewry. We did. A number of us in the round table were more or less radically critical of the Establishment stance. It was all carefully tape-recorded. B'nai B'rith promised to print the whole thing as a symposium. In September 1970 they decided not to, after all, and didn't even bother to call the participants (I found out by demanding to know when it was coming out). And what didn't they want published? For one thing, Rabbı Jay Kaufman, director of B'nai B'rith, explaining morality to the young (and why there were more important things than asking Israel to act morally toward the Palestinian people): "Why, I act immoral in many ways," he said. "I pay my maid less than I ought. I pay taxi drivers in Washington less than what would be a moral wage for them. But that's the way life is." And when I answered by saying, "No, that's the way the Jewish Establishment is: You know what's moral and don't act upon it," the B'nai B'rith response was to strip that whole exchange from the transcript, when they still expected to publish the "edited" transcript. Or another gem from Rabbi Kaufman: If he and a few of his staff stopped working for a year, B'nai B'rith would dissolve. And when I said that meant they were de-organizing the Jewish People, cutting the guts out of the Jewish People, the B'nai B'rith response was to chop all that out of the transcript too.

By early 1971 the atmosphere had grown considerably worse. The Anti-Defamation League of B'nai B'rith issued a public statement denouncing the Medical Committee for Human Rights and the Health Policy Advisory Center as destructive of good medicine, refused to make available to the organizations attacked or to the press the "public report" on which its statement was based, and hinted that MCHR's and Health-PAC's support for community control of hospitals and the health system smacked of anti-

Semitism. How could ADL smell that particular dragon under these particular beds? Because in some big cities—notably New York—the great hospital empires are at least nominally Jewish—though now closely tied to Federal and business bureaucracies. Therefore an attack on their present structure as undemocratic and unhealthful might *in fact,* regardless of formal political ideology, be "anti-Semitic." In any case, ADL felt obligated to defend these Jewish Establishment institutions. On the other hand, it had no interest in the many Jewish medical workers who were involved with Health-PAC or MCHR: perhaps ADL considers them "self-hating" Jews.

Almost simultaneously *Commentary* magazine, published by the American Jewish Committee, editorially recited an abject litany to the White House—divorcing not only itself but the whole Jewish People from the civil rights, anti-war and other insurgent movements of the past decade: "David Dellinger is not Jewish; Tom Hayden is not Jewish; Staughton Lynd is not Jewish, Carl Oglesby is not Jewish; Timothy Leary is not Jewish, Kate Millett is not Jewish; and neither . . . is Stokely Carmichael Jewish, nor Huey Newton, nor Angela Davis. . . . The Movement . . . had a decidedly Protestant flavor, with its tone being set by divines like A. J. Muste and Martin Luther King." And then, admitting there were some Jews in those movements, even some rabbis, explains that they were not really Jewish: They were self-hating Jews. They were anti-Semitic Jews.

How pitiful, how sorrowful! That such a statement, so strongly begging for the acceptance of Jews as trustworthy subjects of the King, itself betrays so deep a fear that the Jews are suspect, are rejected, by those the statement most dearly wants to honor. How pitiful! how sorrowful!

Such a performance may fill us with pity, or with disgust; with anger, shame, or dialogic zeal. But it is important to channel these feelings into knowledge. *Why* this response?

The basic defense of the Jewish Establishment for its

own retrenchment, its own deliberate restriction of vitality, is fear. Fear that the Jewish People is utterly alone. Fear that if we decide that our own tradition in this moment requires Prophetic radicalism, we will be destroyed because we are alone. Fear of the White House. Fear of the Black community. Fear of the Tsar and fear of the peasants. Fear that we live not at a crossroads, a crisis whose resolution might be world disaster or world liberation, Jewish disaster or Jewish liberation—but that where we live is on the brink of disaster. *Only* disaster. Fear that any motion will plunge us into the chasm.

And so for Jews as Jews, quietism. Inwardness. Let us renounce our beacon to the nations, become a small people. The politics this requires? An abject clinging to those Rulers who at the moment have the greatest power. And when the trembling paralysis of will becomes unbearable, an outburst of hysteria—followed by a return to trembling paralysis. At some moments, a fear so overwhelming that those who feel it try to divert the attention of the Rulers with a human sacrifice. "It is those others who are standing firm against you. Not us. Not us real Jews. *Take them*."

Some of the fear, the loneliness, comes of course from being Jews who lived through the period of the Holocaust and were formed by it. But not all. For some (not all) of those who respond this way happen to have been formed by the '40s and '50s less as Jews than as social democrats or as ex-Communists or ex-Trotskyists scarred by their encounters with their parties into becoming social democrats. There was nothing wicked about this, any more than it is wicked for a Jew to become a non-Jewishly identified radical of the New Left. Men form their identities in different ways. What is wicked is contempt for another identity that is not intrinsically oppressive—whether it is some Jews' contempt for those who chose a radical identity or some radicals' contempt for those who chose a Jewish one.

The puzzlement and disbelief of these more-social-democrat-than-Jewish Jews at seeing revolutionaries who define themselves as Jews and feel their revolution as a Jewish one may stem from the fact that they see their own primary community and identity as that of social-democrats-without-regard-to-race-or-religion, not as a Jewish one. So perhaps they project their feelings onto the radical Jews. Obviously their tendency to do this is facilitated by the fact that many of the radical Jews "started" radical and grew into Judaism. But that makes their mistake no less destructive.

They are social democrats for a reason. Facing the country that had conquered half the Earth between 1940 and 1945, they knew in their bones that no one could ever change it from the bottom. So they gave up agitation and insurgency for manipulation. Through the '40s, '50s, and '60s, the social democrats saw themselves as a cadre leading ADA, ADA as a cadre leading the Democratic Party, the Democrats governing America, America remaking the world. Under Lyndon Johnson the dream came true—and proved disaster. When Johnson tried to hand over power to Humphrey, the social democrats' favorite stalking horse, the disaster was confirmed in defeat. And when will those days come again—the days that never quite came once?

Not bloody likely. Something new—much more insurgent—is stirring in the land. Its every success infuriates ex-radicals who gave up on insurgency. Its every failure delights them. Its people ignore them. (The bright and energetic non-Jewishly-identified Jews who would have read *Commentary* in 1961 read the *New York Review* and *Ramparts* now. And the committedly Jewish young Jews read *Response,* sing Carlebach, and wear talleisim to march against the White House. Some even read *Response* and *Ramparts* both!) The social democrats might come back to power, but only as social bureaucrats. Not even ruling from the top. Serving a Nixon, a Muskie.

So they feel alone. Indeed, as social democrats they feel even more alone, even more without allies, even more dependent, than they would if they felt primarily Jewish. And they write large for the Jewish People the role, write small, which they play themselves: clerks for the king.

Those whose identity was formed chiefly as Jews react to the 1960s in a different way. For the 1960s were a period in which the form that the American Crisis took pitted others most directly against the organized Jewish community. Who moved into action during the 1960s? Blacks, Puerto Ricans, and professionals and students who were often Jewish, but if so were rarely members of specifically Jewish organizations.

And against what bulwarks did they move? Against the structures nearest to them. For Blacks, in the South, that meant Southern White structures. But urban Blacks began to move, the structures nearest them turned out to look "Jewish." For example, Blacks moved against the marginal stores operating in the Black communities—stores owned or operated by a higher than "random" number of Jews. Blacks moved against public school bureaucracies staffed by a higher than "random" number of Jews.

The syndrome was an old one. Once again, one of the key oppressions suffered by Jews at the hands of a Western society—this time, America—had been to be slotted into roles that seemed oppressive to the desperately poor. The Jewish grocer might charge Blacks high prices because the non-Jewish bank was charging him high interest—but the Blacks were likely to focus on the immediate oppression. The Jewish teacher might jam suburban English down Black throats because a non-Jewish educational Establishment had jammed it down his own throat—but the Blacks were likely to focus on the immediate oppression. Similarly for Jewish social workers, Jewish doctors. . . . So when the poor began to move— even when that movement ignored or specifically discounted as unimportant the Jewishness of the grocer or the teacher—the targets of the movement saw it as directed against them for their Jewishness. Occasional outbursts of explicit anti-Semitism from some Blacks merely

confirmed the fear that the whole Black movement was se-
cretly anti-Semitic, concealing the fact only for tactical
advantage. So the response was a defensive, anti-Black
upsurge.

The alternative would have been for the Jewish grocers
and teachers to ally themselves with the Black energies
against the social system that had oppressed them all.
Some did—particularly among the young teachers and
young physicians who had more flexibility of thought and
life-style, more leg room in status and perhaps in money,
to shrug off a traditional career. But these were the least
identified with organized Jewish life. Perhaps, indeed, the
younger they were the more they had been deprived by
a low-content Judaism of any opportunity to identify
with it, and so were angriest at the emptiness they knew
in the schuls and bar mitzvahs of their youth. (Their parents had grown up in a Judaism more deeply rooted in
the realities of Eastern Europe.) So those who felt most a
part of organized Jewish life also felt more threatened by
the Blacks—and those Jews who felt most hostile to organized Jewry were also those who were most likely to
welcome the Blacks as allies.

When organized Jewry began to condemn the Black
demands as consciously or unconsciously anti-Semitic, the
Jews who allied themselves with those demands had two
ways to go: accept that they themselves were no longer
Jewish, or indignantly assert that although their lives had
been deprived of Jewish content by the Jewish Establishment, their lives were more "Jewish" in form (and sometimes even in content) than were those of the Establishment that was denouncing them. So some of the
uninvolved young Jews were thrust into Jewish life by the
urging of the Blacks to go home and organize their own
community, and some were thrust into it by the denunci-
ations of their own community's "leadership." Most often
both. Then, when some Blacks did indeed begin to capi-
talize on latent anti-Semitism among some Blacks, some

radical Jews found themselves grappling with *that*—and becoming more Jewish, but no less radical, in the process.

Thus from several streams and eddies of the historic Black-Jew encounter, came three developments: a scornfully non-Jewishly identified wave of Jewish radicals; the radical Jewish movement, who call themselves "radical Jews," created chiefly by newly committed Jews who welcomed Blacks as allies; and a conventional Jewish leadership increasingly fearful of the Blacks (and sometimes seeing as its reference group not the Jewish communities in America but the American Establishment or the Israeli government).

But—as if the encounter of the Black and Jewish peoples was not sufficiently troublesome in itself—it coincided with another scenario—an international one—that often seemed to those engaged analogous, and that strengthened or deepened in the various respondents the different learnings they had absorbed at home. Imagine the whole encounter over again, but this time in Giant dress, and in hostility and danger the equivalent of about forty years further along the vicious spiral—and this time conducted on the nation-state level. With the Israeli government—once flexible and creative and insurgent, but by the late '60s rigid and institutionalized, auditioning for the role of the American Jewish Establishment; Arabs in general and Palestinians in particular seeming to play the part of the Blacks; and the American Empire abroad adopting the role of the American Empire at home. And imagine the added pressure that put on the three groups of Jews—non-Jewishly-identified Jewish radicals, radical Jews, and Jewish Establishmentarians—to push forward their own diverse reactions to the world. Imagine how the sense of impending domestic collision was strengthened by the already achieved Middle Eastern collision—which began to look like a "future history" of the encounter of Black Americans and Jewish Americans. Imagine how the non-Jewishly-identified Jewish radicals "learned" from this quasi-history-of-the-future to wonder whether the very existence of the Jewish People was oppressive; and how the Jewish Establishment learned from it how to line up with the toughest, Greatest Power one could find—against the other exploited peoples. Imagine how the "radical Jews" learned that Jews must, explicitly as Jews, link their liberation with that of other oppressed peoples. And now imagine the agony of fear and fury that has poisoned the Jewish community, trying to cope with its history and future.

What kind of Judaism can heal this fear and fury, bind together all the Jews who take Judaism seriously with all the Jews who take radicalism seriously? We—the celebrants of the New Diaspora, radical Jews, the Jewish "counter-culture"—call us what you will—firmly believe that the only Judaism which can do this *in our generation* is one rooted in those strands of the tradition that command both resistance to idolatry and positive outreaching for the Messianic Age, those strands which look to the day when "Blessed be Egypt my people, and Assyria the work of my hands, and Israel my heritage"—the day of allies in liberation.

And in the 1970s many of us—not all—see the glimmerings of a present possibility, alongside the commandments of an ancient faith. For many of us believe the Pharaohs are as hard of heart, and therefore as weak, as they were when Pharaoh's chariot was plunged into the sea. Many of us believe there *are*, or *are about to be*, allies in the building of liberation—if the Jewish People will take the risk of seeking liberation.

Many of us believe that in the 1970s and 1980s the American Crisis—which is the crisis of the most sophisticated, most advanced, most wealthy, and most powerful society on Earth, and therefore is a crisis of the whole world system—will deepen, not abate. The 1960s were just the first stage of the American Crisis, the first peel of the onion. Those most affected were the outer skins of the onion, the marginal people: Blacks, students, Chicanos.

But now the crisis is starting to cut deeper into the onion.

Why? The substructure of America, what keeps people alive, has been allowed to rot away for a generation while money was put into the Super-War Machine. Sewers are ready to fail, the health system is collapsing, houses haven't been built. The substructure *has* to be replaced, fast, if there is to be internal peace; but it may very well *not* be replaced, because the money is not available unless it comes from the military budget, corporate profits, the middle class, or industrial expansion—and there are strong political reasons why it cannot come from any of them.

If the substructure continues to falter and fail, most workers and suburbanites will see the collapse as clearly the fault of the Establishment, not of Blacks or Yippies. So then it would be the working class and middle class, the inner layers of the onion, who get hurt. Who get furious. Who get moving.

There would be Jews among them—Jews solidly embedded in organized Jewry, not the "marginal" Jews of the movements of the 1960s. And they would be moving not against the institutions where Jews have great stakes, as some of the movements of the 1960s did, but against the real power centers of America—which are not Jewish.

So the Jews, the Italians, the Appalachians, the Poles, could find themselves moving as allies of the Blacks and Chicanos against the Empire, rather than as minions of the Empire against the Blacks.

There are already indications in the politics of the early 1970s that this possible path of future history has begun to be followed. How should radical Jews be responding to the particular oppressions of a more and more destructive social order, so as most effectively to create workable pieces of a new and nondestructive society? Does the fact that the oppressions newly characteristic of the 1970s will be coming down across ethnic lines mean that it is a mistake to organize resistance along ethnic lines, and with a Jewish focus?

Of course there are many aspects of our lives in which

American Jews are oppressed not simply because we are Jews—but as workers and consumers and residents in the same ways that our non-Jewish co-workers and co-consumers and neighbors are oppressed. It is important for a radical Jewish movement to be clear about this, and to raise these issues at the same time it is raising issues of uniquely Jewish oppression. To do otherwise would be to retreat into the worst forms of mere cultural pluralism—which would not in fact liberate the Jewish People. What good would Shabbat be, if for six days of work our lives were utterly alienated and exploited? Indeed, would Shabbat be Shabbat? And this last point is a crucial one: given the holistic nature of the Jewish life process at its best, an economic or military or ecological oppression that affects all Americans in both an individual and a communal oppression for the Jewish People. If the nature of work is so oppressive as to curdle the Shabbat, Jews and Italians and Appalachians will all suffer as individuals and the Jewish People—and perhaps the other Peoples as well—will suffer as a community. Radical Jews cannot, either as a matter of tactics or one of principle, ignore the issues that affect non-Jews.

On the other hand, to abandon the particularly Jewish issues would ignore the nature of the American Empire, would sell out our own belief that liberation must happen in and through real communities—not merely some abstract "human" identity—and would crush our own deep knowledge that one of those communities is Jewish.

The crucial fact about America that we must keep in mind is this: *The Empire has acted so as partly to homogenize and integrate all communities into an atomistic, easily governed mass; and partly so as to preserve just enough differences and separations between various communities as to make it difficult for everyone to move together.* Thus, for example, the Empire has not on the one hand forced all women into the modern industrialized work force on a totally "equal" basis; but it has also not kept all women as separated slaves at home. Similarly with Blacks and Chicanos: they are not *purely* internal colonies, and not *simply* members of the same exploited working class as other workers.

In order to organize effectively and liberate all Americans, we must grasp this doubleness and organize through it, not reject it or pretend it isn't there.

What then are the "nonspecific" oppressions it is important for a Jewish radical movement to address—the oppressions that large numbers of the Jewish People suffer as workers, consumers, residents?

All of us are subjected to poisonous air and water and to the danger of a total collapse of a life-supporting environment of planets, animals, and planet Earth. The danger is universal and the oppression increasingly equally imposed upon all (though the in-workplace pollution of mines and factories is still worse than general environmental pollution). Most of this environmental degradation is done for corporate profit; a great deal is linked to the high-energy, low-labor technology of the War Machine. Many elements of the Jewish tradition support a far more life-affirming, life-protecting politics; it would be urgent for a radical Jewish movement to draw on *and expand on* these elements of the tradition and to ally itself closely with all other movements prepared to resist the corporate-military rape of Earth. It should be made clear to Jews that individual responsibility in this matter requires political responsibility: not just that each family decide to use lead-free gasoline, but that the whole structure of oil-auto-highway complex be remade, and transportation put under the direct control of its users and workers so that transportation can serve life, not destroy it.

All are endangered by militarism, imperialism, and the danger of thermonuclear holocaust. The fact that the Jewish People would not be singled out for destruction by a nuclear war should not blind us to the fact that general thermonuclear war would almost certainly destroy the Jewish People while decimating humanity. On behalf of ourselves and the whole human race, we have an obligation *as a Jewish movement,* not simply as people who happen to be Jews, to end the militarism that is clearly moving toward that result. In the "meantime," while preparing for the Holocaust, modern American militarism saps the freedoms essential to the Jewish People and all other peoples living in America. It provides the physical and political technology and the political back-up for the internal militarism we call repression or a police state. It also provides the technology and back-up for imperialism in the Third World. To all these dangers Jews are especially sensitive; we should organize against the root institutions that feed these dangers.

All Americans suffer from the destructiveness of the "educational" system. But because of the Jewish past, disproportionate numbers of American teachers and students are Jewish. Jews thus suffer disproportionately from the new forms of oppression placed by the American educational system upon all its students, and teachers. The schools and colleges do not teach, they rather train; they do not liberate, they rather dull the mind; they create not citizens but jobholders; they encourage not spontaneity but regularity. Teachers and students are taught to police each other. Radical Jews should be drawing anew upon both the Jewish tradition and the radical vision to break the bonds of present schooling and re-create a free interplay of knowledge and moral reason—as exemplified in the Talmud, itself a kind of seminar notes from a free university.

All Americans, though not to an equal degree, now suffer from the generation-long failure to invest in such crucial needs and services as health facilities, sewage systems, schools, transport, housing, etc. We should be pressing not only for reallocation of resources to these areas but for a tax system that requires the rich to pay for them, relieving the poor and the semi-poor working and middle class from the burdens of much of the present regressive tax system. In addition, we should be trying to achieve direct democratic control over these services to be served by them—rather than by a corporate or political or administrative elite. Thus we should be creating worker-and-community-controlled co-op groceries, not assisting capitalist merchants; starting teacher-and-student-controlled schools, not helping the Downtown Educational Administrators. The Jewish hospital system should be one major focus of our energies in this area. In all this the Jewish tradition is clear. We should be organizing in and through it, and developing its obvious public-oriented thrust in new emphatic ways.

The exploitation of consumers affects us all. The distinction between recipients of "public" services ("clients") and recipients of "private" services ("consumers") must be reexamined by a radical Jewish movement. Why is food not a public service? Should, for example, whole milk and vitamin-enriched soy bread be absolutely free to all Americans? But wherever, and for however long, some form of "private" provision of food, furniture, clothing, etc., etc., is considered desirable, every effort should be made to establish direct public controls to end and prevent the present corporate exploitation of consumers. Direct controls should include local neighborhood, workplace, and ethnic-group control: not the present process of Federal commission review, which constantly falls under the control of the corporations being "regulated."

No seriously radical Jewish movement can ignore these areas in which Jews are oppressed, along with other people, while focusing solely on arenas in which Jews are oppressed as Jews or in special "Jewish" ways. To do so would not only leave Jews unliberated in crucial aspects of their lives, but would mean adopting for our movement a new version of the slogan "Jews at home, citizens outside." We utterly reject any such idea, believing as we do that Jewishness is adequately expressed only through wholeness, and therefore that our movement—as well as fully liberated individual Jews—must be Jewish both "at home" and "outside": both on "Jewish" and on "general" problems.

As the American Crisis deepens, the dangers of inaction multiply. For the Jewish community not to act as the knife cuts deeper into the onion would not only betray Jewish ethical values and the immediate material interests of most American Jews, but also endanger the long-term political position of the Jewish People. Inaction by radical Jews would feed the growth of the Jewish Defense League and similar rightward "defensive" organizations which cannot be answered by conventional Jewish liberalism, and would allow the formerly liberal Jewish community to become a permanent enemy of the liberation of American society.

To act requires not only organizing the growing anger against particular oppressions, but also creating concrete projects that provide nonoppressive alternatives.

We could respond to the crisis of the American health system (to which the Anti-Defamation League responded with a defense of the great hospital empires) with an answer more rooted in the Jewish tradition: neighborhood-based, community-controlled health centers that treat the whole person, psychological and cultural as well as "physical"; centers in which health work and decision-making are shared, and artificial barriers between doctors, nurses, patients, and "nonprofessional workers" are lowered; centers that serve as focal points for political campaigns on issues of pollution, public health, garbage.

We could respond to the conscription of our bodies and our money into a war of the American Empire that is forbidden by our Torah, with the clear withdrawal of the Jewish People in the United States from that war: refusing war taxes, turning our synagogues into sanctuaries (like the six cities in Ancient Israel) for those who have refused their taxes and bodies to the Idol Moloch, denying our brains to the war machine.

We could build urban and rural kibbutzim in North America that embody in the present the dream of a future liberated Jewish People, and then organize toward that dream. Kibbutzim that work in the whole round of production that our people, and North America, need: produce food, industrial goods, child-rearing, sociology, prayer, and poetry. That live not on even the oppressed oppression of others, but on our own work, our own love, our own play.

Kibbutzim in which work itself is liberated, the Shabbat casts its light over all the week, and the kibbutz reaches out to other workplaces, other celebration-places, and other politics-places to transform and unify themselves.

A kibbutz does not begin overnight. We can see the bare beginnings of kibbutzim in the Boston and New York chavurot, in Jews for Urban Justice and The Fabrangen in Washington, in the Radical Jewish Community of Los Angeles, and the *Brooklyn Bridge* in New York. But all these are fragile. Not one is a Production Cooperative, let alone the Full Cooperative of which Buber wrote. We must deepen them, federate them, examine how and why many of the Israeli kibbutzim have been encapsulated and bureaucratized, break through to a better, clearer, kibbutz. We must also recognize that not every Jew in America will see the kibbutz as the form of liberation most appropriate to him or her, and we must encourage the invention of other forms. But to many of us the jumping-off place for our thought and action is clear.

If radical Jews can reach out in these ways to reconstruct our own lives; if we can break out of the "mini-oppressor" roles our real oppressors have slotted us into, and rebuild the seamless whole life process of the Jewish community; if we can reach out to talk with, join with, other men and women who suffer in bureaucracies, who suffer from the two-hour tortured drive to and from work, who suffer isolated in their housewifery, who suffer from the speed-up on the assembly line—to talk and work with them not as racists, sexists, imperialists, not as oppressors, but as the oppressed—as brothers and sisters, not the enemy—we can build the kind of movement that liberates the Jewish People *and* the other peoples. Liberates us, and them, not to abandon our differences but to build upon them in nonoppressive ways.

Avodah Gimel

I—Guidelines for Action
Adopted by Jews for Urban Justice,
November 1969

1. A project must organize Jews, i.e., involve them in a continuing way and constantly deepen their understanding of the needs of America and of the Jewish People. Where to concentrate organizing energy will depend on the situation, particular issues, etc., but— other things being equal—organizing should address various groups in the following order:
   (a) Jews from 23–35 (jobholders with no or very young children, frequently not yet members of a synagogue).
   (b) Jews from about 13–22, in high school and college, often members of a synagogue youth group or of Hillel.
   (c) Other Jews, especially members of a conventional Jewish institution that is involved in a particular action project.
2. The project must be clearly based on a Jewish moral and ethical outlook and must explicitly defend Judaism and the Jewish People from cooptation and corruption at the hands of those who are powerful in American society, as well as from coercion.
3. The project must identify as the basic "enemy" not

the Jewish People but one of the particularly immoral structures of American society and those who rule it:

—for example, the system by which huge food corporations hire migrant farm workers at abysmal wages and charge high prices to housewives, making big profits at both ends;

—for example, the system by which huge banks pay low interest to small savers and reinvest their money with those segments of the economy that need new capital the least but can pay the most for it (i.e., big businesses) while denying it to the poor who need it most;

—for example, the system by which tax money is collected from (chiefly) lower-middle-income people to be refunneled through the military budget to high-profit businesses for making destructive and dangerous products likely to kill precisely the taxpayers who paid for them.

4. The project should if at all possible focus on Jewish institutions that cooperate with these larger, usually non-Jewish structures:

—for example, a Jewish-owned grocery chain that deals in food grown under exploitative conditions;

—for example, Jewish groups that put their money in banks that never lend money to the poor;

—for example, a dominantly Jewish scientific organization that makes new weapons for the war system.

The project must make explicit, however, that Jewish institutions are not the major enemy, and that by ceasing to cooperate with immoral larger structures they would redeem themselves. There may be a few cases in which Jews should be organized to confront directly the larger enemy of No. 3, but usually the power of Jews to effect change will be greater if they focus on Jewish institutions.

5. The project must try to address people who do not

control but are in some way part of the coopted Jewish organization (e.g., customers of a food store, members of an investing synagogue, scientists in a RAND) and should make clear that we regard such people as not even a secondary "enemy," but as potential chaverim. Only if the attempt to get some of these people moving utterly fails shall there be consideration of the possibility of confronting them in an angrier way.

6. The project must propose and if possible should create an alternative to the immoral present system:

—for example, a Jewish co-op store operated in close association with the Farm Workers union;

—for example, direct investment by Jews in business efforts of the poor, Black or "new youth culture" communities (not simply in individual enterprises, but in co-ops, etc.);

—for example, creation of a research group or institute of Jewish scientists doing muckraking research on the military budget, or failures of the Highway Safety and similar government agencies, etc.

7. There must also be projects that look "inward" toward strengthening those Jews who have already been "organized"—for example, seminars or schools in Judaism for them and/or their children, a synagogue, etc. Every effort should be made to have such institutions be radical in process as well as "substance." Thus a Jewish Freedom School should be controlled by the teachers and students; its teachers should encourage self-teaching by the students through joint projects; it should encourage the union of intellect and emotion and of thought and action; it should avoid or resist the traditional textbook and other "big power" educational institutions; and it should explicitly continue to identify immoral American power structures as the enemy of its work.

II—The Fabrangen
A Report by Robert Agus

A Fabrangen is a Chasidic gathering at which stories are told, songs sung, and lessons learned. It was and is the way that the Chasidic culture was transmitted to the far-flung Jews of centuries ago and the even more disparate groups today. Combining the joys of singing, dancing, praying, and learning in an environment of communal warmth and love a Fabrangen not only transmitted but became a living example of the Chasidic culture.

We think that the concept behind the Fabrangen is analogous to the goals of the "Jewish cultural center" so that we have chosen the word as the name for the center. We want our Fabrangen to be a vehicle for "bringing together" (the literal meaning of the word) the widely scattered members of the new generation in order to both experience and develop a richer meaningful Jewish culture. We feel that most of our Chaverim increasingly share in the effort to identify and adopt new value structures. We believe that many sense the need to develop alternative life-styles that reflect the changed values. We think and feel that the creation of truly human communities must be an integral part of both the new culture and its process of creation. We hope that the Fabrangen will become a useful way of working on these challenges.

The Fabrangen, which will be located somewhere near Dupont Circle, will consist of many different aspects all of which hopefully will be related to the twin goals of communal and cultural development. One aspect will be the provision of needed services in the areas of legal assistance, drug counseling, personal counseling, etc. These services will be provided by a core staff and volunteers who will commit themselves to specific time allotments.

The purpose behind such services is to involve both recipients and givers in the process of communal development. Of course at the same time needed assistance will be provided. We anticipate working with such groups as the Free Clinic, Freedom House, the Jewish Social Service Agency, and the Jewish Community Center.

The second aspect will consist of educational, religious-cultural, and social action experiences. We hope that as an integral part of the center a Jewish free university will be created. It would consist of people interested in learning together about different aspects of the Jewish experience—its value and culture—and its relevance to the new cultures. It would also stress the interrelationship between study and action whether in the field of ethics, ritualistic expression, social change, or interpersonal relationships.

Rejoicing in the beauty and mysteries of life, expressing our oneness with all men, all life, all nature, and the Whole; reflecting on the sadness of past experiences and of present feelings of loneliness, fear, and powerlessness; relating to our people of the past and of the future—these are some of the reasons for the inclusion of "religious" experiences. We shall continue the ageless process of synthesizing our traditions with the opportunities of the present. Shabbat celebrations, communal meals, sanctification of the New Moon, cultural activities in music, art, film—all these will be an integral part of the total effect.

Central to the entire effort must be the recognition that a true culture is one that ties together and makes meaningful the diverse aspects of one's life. A Jewish culture is one that rejects any separation between religious and secular (but not between holy and profane), between belief and action, or between the individual and his community. Therefore the Fabrangen must work toward and operate within the context of a wholistic culture. Hence engaging in social action to redirect the energies of our society from death-decreeing to life-enforcing activities must be an aspect of the center's activities.

From the Fabrangen Newsletter:

Friday March 19—Shabbas dinner and tefilot, starting 7 P.M. Try to come early and help cook dinner. Come with a colorful scarf or shirt. Four-cornered shirts—dashikis—with tzitzis are available from our Jewish Garment Factory, excellent for Shabbas joyfulness. Sing! Dance!

Tuesday March 23—Weekly seminar on "Marxism, Anarchism, and Judaism." Bring a copy of Buber's *Paths in Utopia* and Marcuse's *Essay on Liberation*; we will read aloud from them as in Talmud study, stopping to discuss and raise questions whenever we wish.

Wednesday March 24—Silk-screening Workshop 7 P.M., Hebrew class 8 P.M.

Friday March 26—Shabbat! Sing a psalm of justice, taste now the Messianic Age.

Saturday March 27—10 A.M., read and discuss the Torah portion of the week. 2 P.M., Mary Gendler leads a discussion on Women and Judaism. 8 P.M., the film *Goldstein*: the prophet Elijah rises from Lake Michigan to herald the Messianic Age, but no one in Chicago recognizes him. On seeing life in present-day Amerika he freaks out and returns to try later.

Wednesday March 31—Shlomo returns! Four-week discussion/experience in Kabbalah, Mysticism, Chasidism. Sing, meditate, dance in the New Moon.

III—Toward Community-Controlled Jewish Health Centers:
Proposal for a Campaign

1. Health is a need of all American peoples and classes that is *not* being provided by the American Empire, and insurgency on this issue is building—among health "professionals" and workers, in labor unions,

in Third World communities, and in the "middle" class or new working class. The Jewish hospitals (especially in New York City) are mostly super-bureaucratic giant institutions that serve the Jewish community poorly and the poor (the Third Worlders) abominably.

2. For these reasons the health issue is one in which (a) both bread-and-butter needs and emotional-cultural needs of the people are not being met; (b) the liberations of Jews *and* of Third World peoples, *and* of the white working class are all at stake, so that an alliance can be built among them; (c) the Jewish community is "officially" involved; and (d) the Jewish Establishment clearly shares control with allies in the general American ruling class.

3. Models for community-controlled, human-scale health care are being created by Blacks, Puerto Ricans, and the "Free" (or Freak, or Yippie) communities: neighborhood clinics where health work and decision-making are shared, artificial barriers between doctors, nurses, patients, and "non-professional" workers are lowered, and whole-person assistance (psychological and cultural as well as "physical") is available. Many of these free clinics have used churches for space. I know of none that have used schuls or Jewish community centers.

4. The Jewish tradition is strongest in its insistence that a life-serving community is one that fuses "religious," "political," "economic," "cultural," and "family" concerns *into a whole life-process*, instead of separating them in such a way as to create alienated human beings. This commitment seems to lead straight toward the notion of a communitarian "whole person" health center.

5. Suppose, therefore, the Jews demanded the total reconstruction of the Jewish health-and-hospital system into a decentralized network of neighborhood or

workplace health centers—say one-third of them in Third World or white-worker areas, one-third in mixed TW-Jewish or WW-Jewish areas, one-third in all-Jewish areas. In each case, these centers should be under control of the people who use them and work in them—not under control of the "private" millionaires or "public" bureaucracies which provide the money.

6. The campaign for such centers could demand that Jewish doctors, nurses, rabbis, researchers, psychologists, secretaries, students, volunteers, etc. become People's Healthworkers, serving psychological-cultural-religious needs as well as physical needs and teaching the patients as much as possible how to meet their own health and cultural needs.

7. The centers could include music, art, writing, and politics—e.g. serve as focal points for campaigns on issues of pollution, public health, sanitation, garbage, and for "advocacy medicine" against the draft, the health-insurance corporations, etc. They could be centers of radical religious or cultural celebrations of life and health (obviously according to the religious and cultural situations of the users).

8. The movement could demand that schuls and Jewish community centers, B'nai B'rith lodges, etc., etc., make space available for the new Jewish free clinics.

9. As Jewish hospital boards reacted (mostly against, no doubt), the campaign could focus on their alliance with Imperial health institutions. Perhaps there could then be support demonstrations, etc., at HEW in Washington.

10. The campaign might be planned and timed so as to address the Jewish community at those times it is most aware of being Jewish: Passover, Chanukah, Rosh Hashanah-Yom Kippur. Such actions could help restore to these holy days their religious, moral, and political meaning, and redeem them from the

commercialization and institutionalization they have suffered.

Chavershaft, shalom, liberation!

IV—The Oppression and Liberation of the Jewish People in America: Introduction to a Draft Paper

Distributed by Jews for Urban Justice at the Revolutionary Peoples Constitutional Convention in Washington, November 1970

There is a Jewish People. It lives and feels its life across state boundaries, drawing sustenance from the Jewish communities of America, the Soviet Union, Israel, Western Europe, and Latin America. It lives and feels its life across millennia, across the rise and fall of several successive civilizations. It is not simply a religious denomination, and its peoplehood is not even chiefly defined by religion. Indeed, its peoplehood is defined chiefly by its refusal, its transcendence, of the conventional categories of peoplehood. The Jewish People is not political, *or* religious, *or* cultural, *or* economic, *or* familial. It is political-religious-cultural-economic-familial. What characterized its peoplehood best, at its best moments, was the principle of Halacha: the way, The Path; a wholeness and fusion of body, mind, and spirit; of action and ideology; of person and community.

During the last two centuries, the worst oppression suffered by the Jewish People was of course the physical extirpation of one-third of its membership by the Nazi genocide, aided or unchecked by many other governments (not least of them the Roosevelt government in America, which failed to open many avenues of action that could have saved millions of lives, hundreds of communities). But in America, during the past fifty years, the Jewish community has also suffered a deep oppression of a totally different kind: an oppression so subtle and so debilitating that it has felt to many Jews like victory.

The oppression of which we speak is precisely the cracking of the community, the splitting of The Path, the isolation and separation of religious Judaism from cultural Judaism from political Judaism from economic Judaism from familial Judaism. The categorization of a People into boxes.

To much of the Movement that during the past decade has risen to struggle against the Amerikan Empire, defining as "oppression" what we have just described may seem peculiar. There are so many more naked oppressions: the genocide of Vietnamese, the subjection of Blacks, Chicanos, Indians, and women, the exploitation of workers, the poisoning of the air and water on which all of us depend for very life. Yet we believe that in a sense the ultimate oppression, the one that even the most reformist ruling class would boggle at removing, the last-ditch defense of the powerful against the rising tide of popular anger and assertion, is the cracking of community, the spliting of The Path into a maze of category boxes.

To understand the depth of our feeling, we ask our radical sisters and brothers to imagine the offer of a bargain from Amerika to the Blacks: "Accept Amerika fully, and you're in the club. We'll give you proportional representation or better among the affluent; we'll mix you residentially all 'round; we'll let you celebrate King's birthday; we'll even let you keep political ties with Africa, so long as you disband these trouble-making Panthers that seek socialism here, and forget about community control, and take these jive jobs in our bureaucracies. (See? We'll even add a few of *your* words to *our* language!)"

Perhaps the Amerikan Empire cannot do this with the Blacks, and survive as an Empire. *But if it did,* would the bargain be liberation—or oppression? We believe that it would be oppression—and that precisely this has been the status offered the Jewish People.

We are organizing and will organize against that oppression.

This does not mean we seek to restore the Jewish community as it was two hundred years ago. The Jewish tradition has incorporated constant transformation, The Path has been a way forward—not a paralysis. We seek a new Halacha, not the old ones. There is much in the tradition that was either a corruption of its best sense, or a failure to rise to new possibilities. We shall try to avoid both—knowing, of course, that whatever we create will not be perfect.

We call upon the Jewish People to free itself by joining in alliance with others to abolish the American Empire that now oppresses the Jewish People and many other peoples at home, and much of the human race outside. We call upon the Jewish People to join the task of creating a democratic, communitarian, libertarian, and socialist society in America. We believe that a fully socialist society will be one in which many self-governing communities are able to end the alienations of mind and body, of politics from economics, of spirit from work, of individual from collective, and thus to create the new, unalienated person; that these communities will differ freely from each other in the shapes they give to the wholeness they make out of these previously alienated lives; and that among these communities a liberated Jewish People will joyfully take its place. . . .

Would it still be desirable for there to be a Jewish People after a democratic transformation of American society? Is it desirable for radicals to identify themselves as Jews and assume the worthwhileness of Jewish peoplehood in the present, when they are organizing for that transformation?

We say yes. We say it for three reasons: one intrinsic to Jewishness, two intrinsic to radicalism.

First: there are some Jews (not all) who not only strongly feel Jewish but strongly want and intend to remain Jewish for Jewish "religious," "cultural," or "political" reasons—that is, for reasons intrinsic to the Jewish "path." This is self-justifying, so far as Jews are concerned; it should carry justification with it so far as radicals are concerned, for a second reason:

Second: so long as any people, any national grouping, desires to be autonomous, radicals outside that grouping should respect and support that desire *so long as it does not involve the oppression of another people.* That is what socialist self-determination means. Some radicals may carelessly call such a desire "racist," and others may put it down as "cultural nationalist." But it is not cultural nationalism *if* the national liberation is linked to the achievement of world liberation, the abolition of empires, and the achievement of democracy. And it is not racist, *if* it (1) is based not on hereditary inclusion or exclusion from the People, but on choice; and, much more important, (2) is *not* based on superior power or wealth—that is, on domination. Black, Jewish, Chicano, Italian, and Appalachian communities could live side by side in a non-racist way *if* none of them controlled another, or had wealth or income superior to another. That is obviously not the present situation in America; but radicals or revolutionaries should be organizing to make it achievable.

Third: we believe (out of both Jewish and general history) that in fact a multi-communitarian society based on real participatory democracy in decentralized institutions is in fact far more likely to involve and reflect real socialism than a unitary society and State embracing more than 200 million people like the present American state. We believe that any aggregation of that many people living under a single all-embracing government (either administrative-political like the one in Washington, or business-bureaucratic like the one in New York) cannot help but become a monster to itself and all other peoples. We believe that a "revolutionary" replica of this monster would still be a monster. We therefore believe that neighborhood, regional, ethnic, and workplace autonomy and participatory democracy are crucial to creating a real people's socialism; and that Super-State socialism in fact soon degenerates into state capitalism. We therefore believe that the creation and preservation of autonomous Black, Jewish, Chicano, Italian, and Appalachian communities in North America is not a tolerable temporary expedient *but an intrinsically desirable process.*

V—"We Are Coming Home":
Statement of "Brooklyn Bridge,"
An Underground Newspaper Collective,
February 1971

We are coming home. To Brooklyn. Those of us who have moved away and forgotten our birthplace, and those of us who still live here and always dreamed of getting out. We have been running away too long, cutting ourselves off from our roots too long, and it has stunted us. We are coming home to Brooklyn to live, to love, to begin building a new world, and to be Jewish.

Brooklyn Bridge is the road we are taking back home. It is a Revolutionary Jewish newspaper. Jewish, because that is what we are; because our Jewishness plays an important part in shaping our total selves, and in the world we are trying to create we want to be full human beings, not assimilated nonentities; because we have learned—as have women, and blacks, and gay people—that unless we look out for ourselves, we are just as likely to be the victims of oppression in a revolutionary society as we are in this one. Revolutionary, because we realize that playing the roles America forces on us will destroy us as it destroyed our parents; because we see that for our people to be free, all people must be free and the deadly hands of America lifted off our backs.

Our struggle begins at home, with the oppression we face as Jewish people in America. We have been trapped in the buffer-zone between other oppressed peoples and the ruling class; shunted into the bureaucracies of the military-industrial-education complex. The commitment of our people to find meaningful and human work—to build a decent society, as teachers, doctors, scientists—is impossible in obscene America. It only alienates us and is used against us. The age-old oppression of Jew-hating and Jew-baiting is like any other racism, both irrational and calculated at the same time. False myths and stereotypes have been imposed on us for centuries. The idea that assimilation through the "melting pot" will end Jew-hating is a dehumanizing lie. Assimilation means believing those myths and stereotypes. It means being cut off from our own history, being cut off from each other. Attempts to assimilate have led us to self-hatred. But no matter how much we might have effaced our spirit, Jews as a nation remain a reality in America, as much of a reality as Blacks, Puerto Ricans, Chinese, Italians.

Brooklyn Bridge is a voice in the struggle to define ourselves. Organized Judaism and the "Jewish establishment" have failed us. The institutions and organizations created to serve the needs and goals of Jewish People have been co-opted to serve other interests. They represent us as a religion, rather than as the nation we are. Jewish philanthropy no longer aids Jews who need it; Jewish education tones down our people's historic fight to survive and teaches us to be "nice Jewish boys and girls." Our culture has been made rigid in the name of tradition and continues sexist oppression both in religious practice and in day-to-day life. Our synagogues are no longer the nexus of our community, but often only temples of ill-founded self-congratulation.

Brooklyn Bridge speaks to the totality of our lives. Our

Jewishness is only part of the wholeness toward which we are struggling. Our oppression as Jews is only one of the ways in which we are oppressed. The ruling class in America oppresses all people; it denies basic life needs, perverting those needs for profit—in the supermarket, in health, in housing. It destroys the environment and murders people in its wars for profit and power.

As Jewish People we demand our right to self-determination. We will defend ourselves against oppression in every way it manifests itself. We are not naive about the struggle involved in achieving our goals. We hope to ally ourselves with other people who are struggling against the same enemies. However, we remember both our own personal histories and the history of our people in revolutionary movements. We will not sacrifice our own aims or struggle to fight for someone else's freedom. No longer will we efface our Jewishness or deny our needs and interests to fit into any current ideological framework. Our brothers and sisters are those people who treat our struggle with the same respect and fraternity that we give to theirs. We are totally committed to the freedom of Jewish People, and all oppressed people. And knowing our oppression, we know that our struggle is against anyone, "revolutionary" or "reactionary," "Jewish" or non-Jewish who oppresses us, who denies us our right to self-determination.

As Jews we have fully experienced the horrors of genocide, racism, and exploitation. As Jews we carry a vision rising out of our tradition of a radical and inclusive social justice. As women and men struggling to survive in America we know we must destroy sexism, elitism, and all other systems of domination that threaten to debilitate our struggle. We will grow in our struggle and we will win.

Brooklyn Bridge is a collective endeavor. An endeavor to open up a dialogue among our people and to begin building a liberated Jewish community. Join us in our trip back home. Take the *Brooklyn Bridge*.

*VI—The Jewish Campaign
for the People's Peace Treaty:
Organizing Leaflet and Questions
and Answers in Support of the Campaign,
Initiated in March 1971, by Jews for Urban
Justice and a National Committee including Marvin
Braiterman, Balfour Brickner, Shlomo Carlebach,
Paul Cowan, Louis Feldman, Helen Frumin,
Everett Gendler, Bob Loeb, Bill Novak, Michael
Robinson, Sharon Rose, Steven Schwartzchild,
Mike Tabor, Peter Weiss, A. J. Heschel, and others.*

PREAMBLE

We, the undersigned organizations and individuals, are committed as Jews and Americans to live in peace with the peoples of Indochina. We now live subject to laws of the U.S. government that compel our support for a war against the peoples of Indochina, but our beliefs and traditions as Jews impel us to separate ourselves from that war. Moreover, we believe that by creating a vigorous, meaningful, and unalienated Jewish community in America, we will not only be freeing ourselves to live out our deepest needs, but making less likely in the future the use of the power of the United States government in unjust and murderous ways. For these reasons we support the adoption by Jews in the United States of this Joint Treaty of Peace, as well as its adoption by all other Americans.

We ourselves shall beat our swords into plowshares, our spears into pruning hooks; and we ourselves shall undo the thongs of the yoke and let the oppressed go free.

JOINT TREATY OF PEACE

Be it known that the American and Vietnamese peoples are not enemies. The war is carried out in the names of the peoples of the United States and South Vietnam but without our consent. It destroys the land and the people of Indochina. It drains America of its resources, its youth and its honor.

We hereby agree to end the war throughout Indochina on the following terms, so that both peoples can live under the joy of independence and can devote themselves to building a society based on human equality and respect for the ear. . . . (There followed a 9-point Treaty.)

By ratifying the agreement, we pledge to take whatever actions are appropriate to implement the terms of this joint Treaty and to insure its acceptance by the government of the United States.

QUESTIONS AND ANSWERS

Our first discussions of the Treaty in the Jewish community suggest that certain questions are raised fairly often. We who are already committed to the Treaty have answered these questions in several ways. (Sometimes different individuals among us support the Treaty for slightly different reasons.) We thought it might be useful to have these issues out on the table. If you have other questions, please write us.

Q. Well, I'm against the war, of course, but why is it *Jewish* to be against the war?

A1. The most important fact about being Jewish is that Jews ought not to *separate* religious and ethical commitments, on the one hand, from politics or everyday life on the other hand. *Jewishness at its best is a whole life process*, and the war is part of our daily lives. (For example, all of us pay for it through taxes even if we speak out against it.) So if we're committed to being Jewish, then dealing with the war is part of being Jewish—we can't just feel we're Jewish on Yom Kippur.

Admitted, this is Jewishness *at its best*—not the way we

have often practiced it in America. But we think the separation between being "Jewish"—that's for Yom Kippur—and being "people"—that's for all the rest of the time—is one of the reasons our lives are so empty. It's also one of the reasons we haven't stopped the war yet—because we act as if being "Jewish"—that is, having religious and moral commitments about the war—is just something for Moratorium Day, while being "Americans" or "people"—that is, paying for the war and not making trouble—is what we should do all the rest of the time. It's clear now we're never going to stop the war *that* way. So we think that because the Treaty pledges us to be at peace with the Vietnamese people in our daily lives, the Treaty is both a step in reconnecting our whole lives to a sense of being Jewish, and a step toward ending the war. We don't think those two goals are contradictory: we think the war will end a lot quicker if the Jewish People gets itself together, along with other peoples, to end it; and we think the Jewish People will get itself together as a *community with a whole life process* that is Jewish if we try to incorporate peace with the Vietnamese, instead of war against the Vietnamese, into our daily lives.

A2. Jews have good reason to support the whole "Nuremberg idea" which came out of World War II, of preventing war crimes like the ones the Nazis perpetrated on us. Yet here our own government is not only letting things like My Lai happen, but is making a *policy* out of burning whole countrysides from the air, forcibly moving whole towns into concentration camps, etc.

What's worse, that policy makes all of us morally responsible, and some of us maybe even legally responsible, for those war crimes. And Jews, long before Nazism and Nuremberg, had a strong sense of individual and communal responsibility not to do crimes when the state tells us to. The Kings, Emperors, Tsars, Chancellors, Premiers, and Presidents in our long history have shown themselves perfectly capable of "doing evil in the sight of the Lord." Obeying them blindly is like worshipping idols—and one of the main aims of Judaism was to end idolatry. The Talmud says that if a ruler commands one person to kill someone else who is innocent, the person should refuse— even if the ruler threatens to kill him. "For is not his blood as red as yours?" But isn't that what our rulers are commanding us to do everyday in Indochina?

A3. Jews in America have good domestic reasons to want the war ended. We are morally committed to a decent society for all—good schools, good medical care, plenty of jobs, reasonable prices for food and housing. We also benefit from those elements of a decent society, and we are endangered when they are denied to ourselves—or others. But the war is undermining the economy and postponing thousands of schools, health centers, houses. The war also endangers us by knocking loose the foundations of social peace in America.

A4. Jews ought to know better than almost anybody else what it's like to be the victim of oppression by Western society. We've been the victim for two thousand years. Now that the Vietnamese people is getting it in the neck from the same Western society that has oppressed us, we should make common cause with them.

Q. Still, I don't see why I should *sign* as a Jew. Maybe I could sign as a teacher, or a Marylander—something like that.

A1. Sure. You could sign up that way too, and urge your city council, your state legislature, and your work-group organizations to adopt the Peoples' Peace Treaty. *Every bit of pressure helps end the war*, including pressure from your schul, your B'nai B'rith lodge, your Hadassah group. That's one reason to sign as a Jew *too*.

A2. We believe that there really is a *Jewish People* in the United States—not just a collection of Americans who happen accidentally to be Jewish individuals. But we believe the Jewish People ought to be much more a *community* than it is now. We do not want to build national organizations run from the top down to which we turn over our sense of right and wrong and our power to make things happen. We intend to act now in our own communities to end the war and deepen our own lives, as Jews. That is something we can only do for ourselves. For example, we suggest calling up some friends to meet, talk about, sign, and act out the Peace Treaty together—not just getting individual signatures.

If this started to happen—if we created a more organic and more democratic community in the Jewish People—we think it would be harder for the government to get us into another war like this one. Because of the way things are now, a few people in Washington who are in charge of the gigantic war machine have enormous centralized power to decide about war and peace, life and death. If there were organic, democratic, people-centered *communities* all over the country—not just a Jewish one, but all kinds—there wouldn't be so much centralized power in Washington. Communities and groups are much more powerful than scattered individuals in standing up for what's right. If we act directly, in common, to withdraw our own support from the war, that is a strong assertion that we *are* a real community, that the Jewish People is alive and vigorous.

Q. But won't signing this as Jews make Mr. Nixon less willing to give Israel the support she needs?

A1. Mr. Nixon makes up his mind about the Middle East on the basis of what he thinks will most benefit the political and financial interests of the U.S. government and some major private companies. He doesn't support Israel for the reasons most Jews do, and he doesn't support her just to be nice to Jews. If he changes his mind it will be a result of his thinking the situation in the Middle East has changed —not us.

A2. President Johnson used to hint he might be less

friendly to Israel if American Jews opposed his policies in other arenas, and the Nixon Administration may be putting out the same notion. But that's typical political blackmail. Naturally the Presidents want to get support for their programs in any way they can; but the issue is, how do we respond? Is it a good idea to cave in when we're blackmailed, or to have a *strong* response? We think that if we cave in, sometime soon the demands for a pay-off will go up again. So we want to respond to that kind of blackmail by straight-put rejection. After all, Jews founded Israel to help liberate the Jewish People to be *more* free to make our own choices and live the lives we believe in. It would be a great betrayal, and a great tragedy, if we let anyone use Israel as a kind of hostage for our good behavior, so we ended up even less free than we were before Israel existed.

A3. Let's remember that living here in the Diaspora, we have our own obligations to Judaism—just as Jews in Israel have theirs. Those obligations are timeless— they don't stop because of a particular political situation, and they don't just apply to Jews. We have an obligation to struggle for justice and freedom for Israelis, but also for the Vietnamese. Is not their blood as red as ours? Or as Hillel said, "If we are not for ourselves, who will be? But if we are for ourselves *only*, what are we?" It may even be that if we struggle well for the protection of small peoples against attack of the kind the U.S. government has visited upon the Vietnamese, we will be building the kind of international climate in which Israelis and Palestinians—both small peoples—can live in peace without being the victims of more powerful nations. But in any case we have to stop participating in terrible crimes against the whole Vietnamese people and even against their very land—crimes that are being done in our name, with our money.

Q. Say I sign. Even say I get my synagogue to vote for it. What difference will it make?

A. Some of us are planning to organize a special Trees for Vietnam campaign. We feel specially responsible to do this as Jews. According to Torah (Deut. 20:19), "When thou besiegest a city many days to bring it into thy power by making war against it, thou shalt not destroy the trees thereof . . . for the tree of the field is man's life."

And here our money, energy, and brains are being used by the U.S. government for a deliberate policy of destroying the forests of Indochina with chemical poisons, bombs, and napalm fire. The American Association for the Advancement of Science reports that defoliants alone have destroyed 25 percent of the forests just in South Vietnam.

So we think that we are responsible to help restore these forests, and we are beginning a campaign to raise money to give the North and South Vietnamese student groups—the same ones that agreed to this treaty—for reforesting the thousands of acres of trees that our own taxes have paid to destroy. *If you would like to join in the Trees for Vietnam Campaign,* let us know.

Q. Trees for Vietnam sounds nice and Jewish, but isn't it a kind of irrelevant and gimmicky project to be talking about while the war is going on? How will the money be spent?

A. In our Trees campaign we're really going beyond the concept of planting "groves" and "forests." Right now much of the land defoliants have been used on is unfit for the growth of *any* kind of vegetation— rice, fruit, rubber trees, manioc, etc. That means large numbers of people must depend on government food surplus (usually after they have agreed to leave their villages and communities). The herbicides also have their impact on birds, mammals, and fish, not to speak of people. Starvation has become a serious problem in many areas. In addition, an abnormal number of women have aborted and a significant number of malformed babies are being reported throughout Vietnam. A number of scientists have speculated that the future impact of chemicals and bombs on the land is disastrous (in 1968 2,600,000 bomb craters were formed). Unless research, experiment, and attention is focused on this problem, huge, desolate, desert-like areas unfit for human life is likely to result.

The $50,000 we are attempting to raise will have a significant impact on the few experiments and research currently being conducted. We also hope it will focus more attention on the ecology aspect of the War. If the Nixon administration tries to withdraw American ground troops but bomb Vietnam into oblivion from the air the Trees campaign could help build the consciousness necessary for vigorous resistance to such atrocities. (Initial reaction indicates that the money will be very gratefully accepted and used for the purposes mentioned.) For more detailed information on this subject, send for the "Ecocide in Indo-China" packet, $1.00, from Jewish Peace Fellowship, 339 Lafayette Street, New York, New York, 10012.

Q. Isn't the war winding down? Why go ahead with this now?

A. The war is spreading out. It is already the longest war in U.S. history. To quote Hillel again: "If not now, when?"

VII—How to Organize a Radical Jewish Group

1. Talk with yourself. *If you have been working in the anti-war or radical movements,* have you been feeling a tug of early Jewish identity surfacing, and have you been wanting semi-consciously to reexamine how that connects with your radicalism? For example, have you felt some special relation—either more critical or more supportive or perhaps in some strange way *both*

—in regard to Israel than your non-Jewish radical friends have, when you talk about the Middle East? Have you felt the flowering of Black, Chicano, and Indian identities reviving a sense of Jewishness in you? Have you worried over the collision course that Black students and Jewish teachers charted in New York, and felt despairingly that organizing in the Jewish community would be important work—but you didn't know how to do it? *Or on the other hand, if you have had a strong sense of Jewish identity and organizational work,* have you been wondering how this relates to your growing sense that present American society is not meeting—indeed, is crushing—important human needs—including yours? Have you been finding yourself wondering whether Judaism could survive a "revolution" or a great social collision in America? Have you been wishing that the Jewish groups that you're in would do something *as Jews* about the Vietnam War, pollution, repression, racism—and wondering why they won't?

2. If the answer to some of these questions is Yes! call up ten or twelve of your friends. Have them over for an evening. Go around the circle—literally—to talk out how you feel about being Jewish in America, about being radical in America, about being radical *and* Jewish. Raise the questions above.

3. If several of you agree that these issues are important to you, schedule more meetings. Invite other people. Keep talking out how you feel. Get hold of the paper "The Oppression and Liberation of the Jewish People in America" published by *The Voice of Micah,* or other issues of that journal (write to P.O. 19162, Washington, D.C., 20036); or issues of *Response* magazine (another journal of "the Jewish counter-culture": write to 415 South St., Waltham, Mass., 02154); the article by Michael Lerner in *Judaism,* Fall 1969; or *The Freedom Seder: A New Haggadah for Passover* by Arthur Waskow (Holt-Rinehart-Win-

ston in New York or Micah Press, P.O. 19162, Washington, D.C., 20036). Discuss them as take-off points, not statements of "dogma."

4. If a number of you in these discussions begin to agree on where you are and what needs doing, talk about particular actions you might undertake. *For example:* (a) Ask synagogues and other Jewish groups in your town how they use their money in regard to racial justice in hiring their staff, in contracting for a new building, in investing in banks, S & Ls, or businesses that do or don't discriminate racially, etc. (b) Campaign *as Jews* against a major pollution maker in your town, explicitly using and developing the Jewish tradition on preservation of the environment. (c) Create and sustain a group of people who hold a small, communal, radical Shabbat service each week. (d) Create a large public Freedom Seder, or a Kol Nidre service attuned to *social* rather than individual sin. (e) Set up an informal public concert of Yiddish workers songs. (f) Organize a Jewish draft-counseling center with an anti-war orientation. *Etc., etc., etc.*

5. At any point along the way where you want to hear what's going on in other places, give us a call: Mike Tabor, 202/462-1982, can arrange to visit, supply you with a speaker, etc.

*Toward a Revolutionary
Diaspora*

IV

Toward a Revolutionary Diaspora

The "eighty-year crisis" of American Jewry may not seem a major event in the thirty-five-hundred-year history of the Jewish People, even though it looms large in the consciousness of American Jews. After all, one or another Jewish community has discovered before, and sometimes with a deeper shock and more brutality, that it did not want to "enter," fuse into, one or another melting pot. But what of the other two crises that link with it—the one that is as major as the Diaspora is old, because it stems from the existence of the state of Israel; and the one that is as major as the People itself is old, because it confronts the question of humanity's survival? These are certainly major events.

First: For the first time since the destruction of the Second Temple, a large and self-governing community of Jews has settled in Eretz Yisrael. But that has created several poignant facts, at least among the young. In 1967 if not before, the Jewish community in Israel proved to be in some sense "ours." But by 1970 if not before, Israel turned out to be not truly "Zion"—that is, not the Hill, the Center from which the Teaching was going forth. No, Israel as well as the Diaspora lived in *galut,* in "exile"; *galut* was indeed spiritual, not geographic. Until the Messianic transformation of the world, Israel would be a state much like other states.

Psychologically most important of all, the very existence of Israel meant that the Diaspora was no longer, if it ever had been, a "necessary evil." For nineteen hundred years it had been viewed this way, and the identity of the Diaspora had been organized partly around the proclamation—usually not expected to be fulfilled in real

127

historic time—of "Next year in Jerusalem." But in our generation the proclamation, taken as a geographic-political statement, no longer had any meaning: in theory, at least, it was no longer "necessary" to stay in the Diaspora; and therefore, in theory at least, if the Diaspora were to survive it could not be viewed as an evil. There were only three possible responses to the proclamation: go *this* year to Jerusalem; stop making the proclamation—that is, stop being Jewish; or reinterpret the proclamation in a nongeographic way. The first two responses meant the death of the Diaspora; the third meant its reaffirmation in some new way.

In this matter, as in most issues of Jewish identity, the theory has done a great deal to influence feeling. For many of the younger Jews of the Diaspora found themselves asking, what does it now mean to be Jewish in the Diaspora? (Their elders continued to operate according to habit.) They felt that being Jewish in the Diaspora could not mean dismissing, disregarding, Israel. It could not mean the total, uncritical acceptance of Israel as Zion. To those who were most serious about their own commitments, it could not even mean viewing Israel from afar as "The Center" of Jewish existence. For, if Israel were truly The Center, one should go there; and if Israel were not "a focus" but The Center, then the Diaspora must be a shadow. No shadow can create anything real. And so the psychological reality emerged that Israel-*centered* Jews must go there if they were to be real and create reality, while Jews who intended to stay in the Diaspora must commit themselves to a belief in the Diaspora as a *positive good*, if they were to make themselves and their community real.

So some young Jews began to see the Diaspora and Israel as two sides of the coin of Jewishness. Without *either*, the Jewish people would not be whole or healthy —not even as whole and healthy as it is possible to be short of the Messianic transformation of the world. Yes, the Jewish communities of the Diaspora were living in *galut,* in alienation; but so were the Jewish communities of Israel. The alienation, the exile, was perhaps less now that there was an Israel, for the existence of the state permitted the ancient creative tension in Judaism between particularism and universalism to be played out in a new way: now there was a self-governing "particular" to wrestle with the universal mission, give it new concreteness and real flavor.

But would it not be equally true that without the Diaspora, the universal thrust of Judaism would be seriously weakened? If all the Jews migrated to Israel, or if all the Jews who did not migrate stopped being Jewish, would the citizens of Israel remain "Jewish" in any important way? Would not their everyday particular concerns, and the absence of any world Jewish People to which they felt connection, soon result in the "Israelization," the "assimilation" of not simply many or most of them, but of them all? Would not even those "Jewish" communities in Mea Shearim and the kibbutzim soon wither away, and the Israelis find themselves a minor tribe—spiritually as well as politically impotent? Would not the "normalization" of the Jewish People as a nation wholly enclosed within its own territory, the stated goal of many modern political Zionists, mean precisely an abandonment of the fruitful Jewish "role" or "mission"?

There are two major arguments against this view—one religiously traditional, one political. The religious argument is that great new spiritual contributions of Judaism cannot require a Diaspora, since the historic spiritual advances were made in Eretz Yisrael before the Diaspora. But that is simply not true, by the Tradition's own testimony. Why does the Torah tell us that Abram's first breakthrough, his denial of idolatry and his first conversation with the God that was no idol, came not in Eretz Yisrael but outside it? Whether we take this as simply a news report or as instructive myth, is it not important that the first assertion of Jewish peoplehood was thus described as a kind of "Diaspora" event both geographically and in the sense that the discovery of God came in response to the alienations of Diaspora life? Again, would there have been a Sinai if there had been no Diaspora in Egypt, or was it not precisely the alienations of the Diaspora that taught Moses and the People what they had to know in order to break through to the Torah? And why not in the land itself—why at *Sinai*—midway between Egypt and Eretz Yisrael—if not to emphasize the importance of the Diaspora? And yet again, would there have been a Talmud if there had been no Diaspora in Babylon? To skip a thousand years—would there have been a Maimonides, a Baal Shem Tov, a Buber, without the Diaspora? Religiously and historically, the Diaspora seems not merely important but indispensable.

The political argument some have made against the continuation of the Diaspora is that the universal mission is too burdensome, the role too heavy, the blood too profuse that has flowed from the universalist Diaspora; and that therefore it is better the Jews become a "small people," abandon the Covenant, and indeed become "normal" at the cost of becoming unimportant. The political hope that lies behind this vision is that once wholly normalized on their own territory, the Jewish-People-become-Israelis could survive. (The religious rationalization for this politics is that the Holocaust canceled the Covenant anyway, that God is dead or very crazy, and that the Jewish People had better look out for itself—itself alone.) But—even if the history of the state led us to believe that it could easily achieve peace with its neighbors—what reason have we to believe that the next rampage by a super-state will leave the Middle East unscarred? Hitler's "conventional" adventures barely stopped short of the Nile Valley, the Suez Canal, and Mandatory Palestine; if the new, post-Hitler super-states begin flinging H-bombs at each other and their allies, what is to prevent American or Soviet H-bombs from annihilating that small territory called Israel? Is there really any safety for the Jewish People in retreating to one small—and, it turns out, highly strategic—corner of the globe, while the super-states remain?

No. It seems far more likely, from the point of view *either* of the survival of a committed Judaism, *or* of the survival of the Jewish People as a physical entity, that the Diaspora is important, is a good in itself. Not simply a necessary evil, but a good in itself.

Because it has a role, a mission. A role, a mission, that emerges from both politics and religion, that directs itself to both physical and spiritual survival. To understand this role, we must look more closely at the third crisis: the "thirty-five-hundred-year" crisis imposed on us by the Holocaust and Hiroshima.

They belong together. For Hiroshima posed the same threat to all of Humanity (including the Jewish People) that Auschwitz posed to the Jewish People specifically. To the Jews, World War II was a threat of the physical destruction of the Jewish People; to the whole human race, it threatened the Universal Holocaust. But these twin terrors were more than simultaneous in time: both stemmed from the same demonic Organization of a potentially fruitful technology. Hiroshima was a demonstration of how to put together the high destructive technolgy on a physical level, without the knowledge or involvement of much of the society; the Holocaust, a demonstration of how to mobilize the whole society for destruction with only a "conventional" industrial physical technology. Now the United States and the Soviet Union are proceeding to merge the two approaches: mobilizing the whole society into a post-industrial physical technology. Together, the two approaches make the destruction of the human race perfectly feasible; and thus the Soviet and United States governments become the most dangerous institutions in human history.

But once such a technology is at hand, it is usable alternatively for the creation of the decent society. And thus Hiroshima and the Holocaust become, perversely enough, indices of the new possibility of transforming the world into decency—rather than death. Into freedom, rather than necessity. Into the Messianic Age, rather than the Flood of Fire. And indeed, both are statements that either the transformation will come, or destruction will.

Among many Jews, the twin message got lost. Some focused on Auschwitz as if no other people were in danger, and as if only an attack directed solely at the Jewish People endangered the Jewish People. Some focused on Hiroshima as if all the differences between peoples had been annihilated in that blinding flash.

But the truth is that both Auschwitz and Hiroshima threatened the Jewish People and that both threatened all peoples of the Earth. Auschwitz threatens all of us in our differences, Hiroshima threatens all of us in our samenesses.

But Hiroshima also threatens us *as Jews,* because *as Jews* we are commanded to build the Days of Peace and Justice, and not to permit the destruction of ourselves and all the Earth. *As Jews* we must do the work that Jonah did in Nineveh—if indeed we live in Nineveh. *As Jews,* we must work to bring the Messianic Age.

Indeed, to some of us, the whole issue of Jewishness now centers on whether the Jewish People, especially in the United States and the Soviet Union, can deal in this coming generation with what will be the most epochal choices of human history. After producing and following Isaiah, if we cannot act to enact his vision: if in this crisis we side with the Idols of the State or take no hand in saving ourselves and Humanity, we believe we will have made a joke out of thirty-five hundred years of the Jewish tradition, or mission, or role.

We do not believe the thirty-five hundred years were a joke, and do not intend to let them become one, if we can do otherwise.

And that is why the three crises now fuse into one for the Jews of America. The first crisis: the mental and emotional exodus from the American Empire. The second crisis: the mental and emotional journey toward the

Diaspora as a good in itself. And the third crisis, which provides the pillar of cloud and fire that calls us onward: the great liberation. Of ourselves to be ourselves, of humanity to be itself.

That is why some young Jews come to believe that *in this generation* of our history, Judaism itself requires us to be revolutionary. Not that the Jewish tradition is always and universally revolutionary. It is not. Under most circumstances, the Talmudic rule *Din malchut din,* "The law of the kingdom is law," has applied. But the Talmud also tells the story of the man who came to the rabbis: "The governor of the city has commanded me to kill an innocent man, and threatened to kill me if I do not. What shall I do?" And the rabbis replied: "Is not that man's blood as red as yours? It may even be redder than yours! You must not kill him." So we learn that on the laws of the earthly king there is a limit: not on any minor pretext, but on certain central issues of God's law they must be disobeyed.

And is this simply a matter of particular laws, or could it ever go to the heart of the whole political system? Let us consult the daily prayers:

"V'la malshinim al t'hi tikvah. . . . Umalchut zadon m'hayrah t'aker utshaber utmager v'tachneah bimhayrah v'yameynu.

"May You bring to nought the hopes of the slanderous informers. . . . May You speedily uproot the Empire of Arrogance and crush it, subduing it quickly, in our own day!"

Thus the nineteenth benediction of the Shemoneh Esreh, the "Eighteen Benedictions" of the daily service. The nineteenth benediction because it was added, long after the others, at the direction of Rabban Gamaliel II, head of the Sanhedrin at Yavneh. Added at the end of the first century of the Common Era, when the Empire of Arrogance was Rome. Added because even at nonrevolutionary Yavneh, even when the first wave of Jewish revolutionaries against Rome had been crushed and the

Temple destroyed, even then the hope of revolution, of the crushing of the Empire "in our own day," was kept alive. Added because above all, there was to be no hope, even from Yavneh, for those slanderers who informed upon the Jewish revolutionaries to the Empire.

What a clearly, vigorously "political" statement to be preserved alive in the liturgy even till our own day! Who reading it can help but know that Judaism is indeed intrinsically "political," and that under some circumstances the most honored upholders and developers of the tradition have called or hoped for revolution? Almost by itself, even if there had been no uprising against Pharaoh, no uprising against Antiochus, no Book of Jonah with its explicit command to preach the imminent destruction of a "violent" city that was not Jewish and was not even oppressing Jews—almost by itself, the deliberate insertion and preservation of the *malshinim* benediction would deal with the claim that Judaism absolutely prohibits a radical stance against the reigning authorities. When Pharaoh makes slavery unbearable, when Antiochus profanes the Temple, when Hitler tortures the Warsaw Ghetto—then a radical response is necessary.

Some Jews believe that we live today under kings like Pharaoh, Antiochus, the Ninevan—and that the potentiality is clear of Hitlers worse than Hitler. There are some who scornfully dismiss that belief. But ought we to trust that the thermonuclear arsenals commanded by the United States and the Soviet Union—arsenals clearly large enough to destroy the human race—will not be used? What state in human history has not ultimately used the most advanced weapons available to it? Ought we to trust that deterrence works forever—not for a decade, not for a century, but *forever*? What arms race in human history has *not* ultimately ended in a war? Are we supposed to forget that the magnificent nineteenth-century balance-of-power deterrent system in Europe ended, after many a success that "proved" its worth, in 1914?

And that is to leave aside the destruction of the world

environment, proceeding in relative slow motion rather than one great cataclysmic scene.

Can the Jewish People survive a thermonuclear war? Can the Jewish People survive the making of Earth unlivable? Simply because all other peoples are threatened along with us, are we the less threatened—and are we therefore the less required to respond?

Suppose we do respond—Jewishly, radically. Suppose we respond that the very structure of the modern superstate is what requires it to threaten the world, and that the inward structure of Judaism provides an answer. A communitarian answer. An answer that requires the building of a new society and the dismantling of the old —with loving care, so as to prevent damage to people, but with thoroughness in the dismantling.

But is any true dismantling possible? Or would the society that follows be as much a monster as the one we live in, if not more? Indeed, the skeptics ask, how can we improve on the history of the Jewish Labor Bund—those revolutionary socialists who in Eastern Europe from 1897 on were committed to the liberation and preservation of the Jewish People where it lived, and who helped make the revolutions of 1905 and 1917 against the Russian Empire? The Bund failed to make a revolution that liberated the Jewish People; indeed, the new revolutionary government itself became anti-Semitic. How can we do better?

To which some answers:

First, anti-Semitism survived in the Soviet Union because oppression survived there too. The revolution was not fulfilled, the Jewish People neither ended their own oppression nor ended their special middleman dependence on the oppressors. The Bund failed: perhaps partly because it was too state-socialist and did not build kibbutzim or in other ways create unshakable power at the grass roots; perhaps partly because it rejected as irredeemably reactionary the religious celebration which is part of what makes the Jewish People and which is at its best an assertion of the human spirit against idolatry and tyranny. But mostly because it was impossible to succeed.

For before our day, no society in human history has been rich enough to be fully free. It would have been very hard for Russia in 1917 to liberate her peasants to be full citizens: they might not have had the time to grow food if they had taken the time to grow human. Perhaps, then, the process by which every revolution has ended in a new ruling class, and some revolutions have therefore ended in some new oppression of the Jews, has been inevitable. But now! Now we live in the era of abundance, the era when no one need be a slave in order that others can have the leisure to govern, the era when all *could* share in governing themselves, if the abundance were shared equally among them. We have achieved that era precisely in the countries that through the power of their maldistributed abundance now rule and threaten to destroy the world. And the abundance itself, in both its good and evil aspects, has provoked a crisis which could be made to result in the transformation of those countries, and therefore of the world.

So now the conditions exist that make it possible—barely, but possible—for us to break through to the "era of freedom," the Messianic Age; and it would be as great a disaster to fail to try with all our strength to bring "Messiah" when the time is ripe, as ever it was to follow false Messiahs when Messiah was impossible. Never before could the human race be destroyed; never before could it be liberated. So also for the Jews.

Our tradition teaches us not only the goal but also the method: to bring the Age of Shabbat, the whole Jewish People must celebrate two Shabbatot in a row. Two meanings: First, it is *we* who are obligated to act—all of us. Second, it is living forth in the present what we foresee as the future society of Peace and Justice that will make the future real. The only means we may use are those that partake of the ends themselves, and to reject illegitimate means is not to postpone the revolution but to bring it nearer.

What does this teach us? That we need to imagine clearly the Jewish People as we would have ourselves be, and then act to create in the present the community we imagine for the future.

A Judaism that is new, but is woven partly from at least five strands of our history: the Prophets in their daring stance against the kings and their commitment to the real transformation they envisioned in the Days of the End; the Chasidic movement, in its transcendence of the "rational-bureaucratic" and its democratization of the mystical experience, its infusion of the everyday with wonder and ecstasy; the Bund, with its deep concern for a large-scale industrial working class and its ability to fuse a Marxist analysis of history from the standpoint of the struggle to end exploitation with its own deep experience of Jewish peoplehood; the kibbutz, with its anarcho-communitarian implication and its creation of a democratically based Halacha; and Buber's existential Judaism, with its grasp of the Dialogue between God and Mankind and its fusion of Anarchism, Marxism, and Judaism into a working politics.

A Judaism, and a Jewish People, that pursues the basic principle of Halacha—the principle that life is a Path, a Way, indivisible, in which politics, religion, economics, culture, the family are fused. Pursues that principle even if the particular codification of Halacha in the *Shulchan Aruch* is not the form taken by the new Halacha (or perhaps by several *halochot*). Our new Way will consist of the same basic elements as the old: i.e., love of life, respect of all Nature, the encouragement of individual development within a communal context, an active passion for social justice and human equality, a recognition of human potentiality. However, it will also be framed in the context of the realities of our day: i.e., it will explicitly deal with the potential destruction of the world environment, of the whole human race, and of whole peoples. It will transform the relations between the sexes, and end the exclusion of women from the central celebrations and governance of Judaism. It will recognize the new fact that the leisure of one human being does not require the slavery of another, and thus will act to fully and equally share the wealth of the world.

The new Jewish community that we foresee, built upon these principles, will be one organized along many different lines. Some may form themselves into *chavurot* (fellowships) of maybe fifty to one hundred each; each *chavura* will be unique, but all will practice some degree of communality as well as strong participation in the expanding Jewish culture. Others may form kibbutzim where the collective will live together and work together in the whole range of production: agricultural, industrial, service, artistic. Others will form larger new communities which might be the homes of Jewish neighborhoods, factories, universities. Others may live and work within the larger community but still involve themselves in Jewish cultural life through participation in the educational and celebrational activities. The entire community would be knit together *from the bottom*, without bureaucracies, by the federation of its various face-to-face communities and the exchange of delegates who do not become a special staff or class. There grows, in short, a kind of plural Jewish Commonwealth in North America—scattered in space but linked by commitment, alongside other Commonwealths created according to real identities—some ethnic, some sexual, some regional, some economic. Ultimately, we imagine the shattering of the American super-state and the radical decentralization of power throughout the continent, as these Commonwealths grow in commitment and in democratic power. Ultimately, we see the emergence of a democratic, ecstatic, libertarian, communitarian, socialist Judaism.

We do not believe these changes can be accomplished in isolation in America. We do not believe, for example, that the American super-state can be abolished while the Soviet super-state remains untouched; for the threatening existence of the one protects the threatening existence of the other. We look toward a process of change in the Soviet Union that revives a sense of independence and the capability of self-government among its peoples and workers too. Among the Jewish People in the Soviet Union now, as in 1905, this kind of rebellious consciousness seems further advanced than among some other parts of Soviet society; and we belive it is important for the liberation of all peoples in the Soviet Union and elsewhere, as well as for the Jews specifically, for the Jewish People elsewhere to aid the Jewish People in the Soviet Union to win more freedom.

Particular attention should be paid to seeing that Soviet Jews who want to create cultural and political autonomy for themselves where they now live should receive as much public support from American Jewry as do those Jews who wish to live in Israel; for almost all the Western focus since 1969 has been on supporting the right of emigration, rather than on autonomy. The tendency of the American Jewish Establishment to denigrate the Diaspora and treat Israel as the central reality of Jewish life is bad enough as it regards American Jewry; it should not be allowed to extend to Soviet Jews as well.

It is also important to avoid strengthening the Cold War in the process of supporting Soviet Jews against the Soviet Empire. The tendency of Establishment-sponsored and right-wing campaigns for Soviet Jewry to celebrate the "freedom" of American Jews as a contrast to that of Soviet Jews must be resisted—not only for the sake of truth, but because it fuels a Cold War view of the world. The liberation of Soviet Jews requires not a new Cold War, but the opposite—a relaxation of tensions between the Soviet and United States governments, in order to allow more play to the domestic insurgencies that could transform Soviet society.

As energy grows in Diaspora communities toward taking the Diaspora seriously as a good in itself, toward accepting for the Jewish People the task of struggling alongside other peoples for its own and the world's liberation, and toward creating newly-halachic communities, these communities—more and more governing themselves, feeding themselves, teaching themselves according to their own perception of the Jewish Path—would necessarily be a threat to the American and Soviet Empires. For such communities could not be the Empires' accomplices or pawns in deforesting Vietnam, occupying Czechoslovakia, keeping people starving in the midst of plenty, locking Israelis, Egyptians, and Palestinians into a permanent arms race punctuated by explosions of death, storing up the bombs to burn the Earth, poisoning the air and water—to name only cases where it is not we alone who are the victims. A fortiori, a newly halachic Jewish People could not be accomplices if the Empires and their clients singled out the Jews to suffer oppression. We would have to resist in both kinds of situations, in order to be ourselves. Such communities could scarcely be "retreatist" enclaves, and when the Empires tried to smash them they would need help from Jewish communities elsewhere.

But the strongest defense for the new revolutionary Diaspora communities will have to come from themselves and their comrades in the Empires themselves. In America as in the Soviet Union, there are many oppressed peoples who have moved, will move, alongside the Jewish People. None of us has moved enough, and we must create new ways of moving.

How can we and the other peoples move? Partly as peoples, out of our own ethnic consciousness of similar oppressions. But partly as workers—in America, for instance, moving from our shared knowledge of the inflation/unemployment oppression, the health/pollution oppression, the bureaucracy/speed-up oppression that American workers are now rediscovering. As workers anywhere, sharing the power workers have: the power to stop working.

For there are the barest hints that from what happened in France in May 1968 and from what happened in

America in May 1970 and from what happened in Czechoslovakia and Poland during the same years—the workers of the world are now remembering the power that inheres in refusal to work for the system. Remembering that political power can grow out of something other than the barrel of a gun. Not elections. They are too slow, a maze to calm and channel sudden floods of popular energy, or simply an elaborate way of collecting the power of the people and handing it over to someone else.

What then? New lips begin to shape an old phrase in a new context: "general strike." Not planning. But remembering, wondering, imagining. Realizing that a "general strike" need not be really a work *stoppage*, but could be a *redirection* of work: that for such a general strike workers need to understand how to run their own factories, farmers how to get food directly to people in the cities so people won't starve, and so on. Realizing that it takes knowledge, comradeship, and hard work to build the alternative future in advance. Remembering, and building on, the workers councils that have appeared spontaneously in almost every revolutionary moment— only to be crushed or disappear thereafter. Remembering, and improving.

We have our own tradition in this matter. The Shabbat was the first general strike, a holy general strike. Let us build an Age of Shabbat!

Avodah Daled

I—Poem/Leaflet
Handed to People Boarding a Bus
For the Dedication of the
"Jewish Community Center of Greater Washington"—
in Montgomery County, Maryland
June 15, 1969

THIS IS THE BUS TO AUSCHWITZ.
At the other end is a building for the destruction of the
    Jewish people—showers, baths, and all.
Think twice before you get on.

It's a soft Auschwitz, of course.
They won't be stripping your bodies and gassing your
    lungs. They'll just be stripping your Judaism and
    gassing your minds.
There's an Olympic swimming pool and a microscopic
    library. Is that likely to create Jews? The Jews of
    scholarship?
There's plush—you wouldn't dream there was a poor
    man for 60 miles in any direction. Is that likely to
    create Jews—the Jews of the Prophets and the kibbutz?
There's a membership list already closed on the day it
    opens. Is that likely to create Jews—the Jews of the
    Chasidic communities?

The "owners" of the Jewish Community Center are not
    interested in creating Jews.
They want to create conformists.
They worship Power, not God—Baal, not Adonai.
But Power is not our God.
Conformity is not our God.

If you get on the bus to Auschwitz, better recite what
the Jews of Auschwitz recited before they died:
Shema Yisrael, Adonai Elohanu, Adonai Echad. Hear,
O Israel, the Lord our God, the Lord is *One*.
Remember that.
Don't die.
Resist dying.
The Lord is *ONE*.

II—Leaflet and Liturgy
CHASE MANHATTAN PLAZA,
Passover 5730—April 20, 1970
Led by the National Jewish Organizing Project

WHO ARE THE AMERIKAN PHARAOHS?

THE ROCKEFELLER EMPIRE is one of the biggest.

We are here to tell the Amerikan pharaohs: LET OUR
PEOPLES GO!
We are here to tell the Rockefeller empire:

FREE US FROM THE GASOLINE FUMES
YOU POUR INTO OUR AIR!

Gasoline fumes are a major source of air pollution.
The Rockefeller family controls Standard Oil of New
Jersey, Mobil Oil, Standard Oil of California, and
Standard Oil of Indiana, which rank 2nd, 9th, 12th, and
17th respectively, on the *Fortune Directory of 500
Largest Industrial Corporations* (by sales) in June 1968.
Through interlocking directorships in the Rockefeller
Foundation, the Rockefeller Brothers Fund, Rocke-
feller University, and the Chase Manhattan Bank,
Rockefeller interests *control* General Electric, United Air-
craft, Boeing, General Motors, Goodyear, Uniroyal, Pan
American Airlines, American Airlines, Eastern Airlines,

Northwest Airlines, and United States Steel. And the Rockefellers' "clean air" branch—Laurence—asks us to pay with our taxes, to clean up the air their profits poisoned.

FREE US FROM THE POISONOUS OIL YOUR COMPANIES SPILLED INTO THE SEA!

Chevron Oil refineries have spilled thousands of barrels of oil into the Gulf of Mexico, ruining hundreds of miles of Louisiana coastline. The beaches of Tampa and St. Petersburg, Florida, are threatened by more than 10,000 gallons of oil from the tanker Delian Apollon, which is owned by Humble Oil and Refinery Company. Both of these companies are subsidiaries of Standard Oil. The Oil Lobby has been successful to date in preventing passage of legislation making operators liable for such damage.

FREE OUR NEIGHBORHOODS FROM THE PYRAMIDS YOU HAVE BUILT UPON OUR HOMES!

The Rockefellers have built and own large chunks of Manhattan: Rockefeller Center, Lincoln Center, Columbia University, Rockefeller University, Chase Manhattan Plaza. These monuments to the almighty dollar were built on the homes of thousands of families who were forced by continued housing shortages and high interest rates to crowd even more tightly into tenement housing. So was the State Office Building in Harlem that Governor Rockefeller jammed down the peoples' throats.

FREE US FROM THE USURY THAT KEEPS US FROM PURCHASING NEW HOMES!

It is more profitable for the Pharaohs to invest in corporate giants that build the war machine or in the Federal government that uses it, than it is to lend money to families to build homes. The result is super-tight money and interest rates that have doubled in twenty years.

FREE US FROM THE SUBWAY FARES THAT GO TO LINE YOUR POCKETS!

The people of the city of New York have paid for the subway system twice already! At the turn of the century Chase Manhattan was among a number of banks which bought $100 million of municipal bonds to pay for the construction of the IRT and BMT. During the Depression these lines suffered greatly from lack of maintenance and loss of ridership. In 1940 the city bailed them out by exchanging the original bonds for $310 million in new bonds. Today these banks collect $65 million a year in tax-free interest payments for money they "loaned" to the transit system. When all the interest is paid, the people will have spent three to four times the original amount borrowed. And we are asked to believe that increased fares are due to increased labor costs!

FREE US AND THE VIETNAMESE FROM THE WAR YOU HAVE SPONSORED BETWEEN US!

Governor Rockefeller has provided much of the crucial political support inside the Republican Party for the War Against Vietnam—from which his family has profited in sky-high interest rates, in business for Pan Am Airlines flying to and from Vietnam, in selling fuel oil for thousands of bombing raids over Indochina, and in business for the Saigon branches of Chase Manhattan.

FREE OUR BROTHERS AND SISTERS OF THE ARAB WORLD FROM THE PROFITS YOU TAKE FROM THEIR LAND AND LABOR. . . . FREE OUR BROTHERS AND SISTERS OF ISRAEL FROM YOUR MACHINATIONS IN THE WHITE HOUSE!

Why does David Rockefeller feel called upon to advise the State Department on U.S. policy in the Middle East? Because he knows that U.S. policy always is geared to keep in power the regimes that will do nothing to challenge the U.S. monopoly on Middle East oil, the regimes that will support U.S. imperialism in Asia and Latin America. Rockefeller oil companies own 70 percent of the oil production of Saudi Arabia, 22 percent in Iran, 58 percent in Libya, and 24 percent in Iraq. The people of these countries are slaves to this imperialism while the ruling cliques deposit millions in kickbacks from U.S. companies in Swiss banks. Meanwhile the Rockefellers invest heavily in the Israeli economy in such a way as to support the most hawkish Israelis. At one moment they may seem to throw their support to the Arabs, at another to Israel; but at every moment they are encouraging the governments and rulers of both to fight each other and are opposing every hint of basic social change on either side.

FREE OUR BROTHERS AND SISTERS OF SOUTH AFRICA FROM THE FASCIST REGIME YOU PROP UP!

In 1960 the Black ghetto of Sharpeville rebelled and was brutally suppressed by the Nazis who run the South African government. An economic crisis followed, but the International Monetary Fund, World Bank, and James Stillman Rockefeller's First National City Bank granted credit to South Africa to pull it through. First National City and David Rockefeller's Chase Manhattan cooperated in a revolving credit of $40 million set up by eleven U.S. banks. The credit was negotiated by C. Douglas Dillon's *Dillon, Read and Co*. Mr. Dillon is a director of Chase Manhattan.

FREE OUR BROTHERS AND SISTERS OF LATIN AMERICA FROM YOUR PLANTATIONS AND REFINERIES!

Venezuela is the world's largest oil exporter and third largest producer. Oil accounts for about 86 percent of the country's export earnings, and 63 percent of the government revenues. Creole Petroleum Corporation, a Jersey Standard subsidiary, owns 41 percent of Venezuela's oil and accounts for a third of Jersey Standard's profits. In 1966, the total net sales of Standard Oil of New Jersey was $12.2 billion, the gross national product of Venezuela was $7.9 billion. Yet, only 1.1 percent of the Venezuelan labor force is employed in the oil industry, while unemployment in the country approaches 20 percent.

THE POWER OF THE PEOPLE IS RISING! THE WRATH OF THE LORD IS GATHERING! WE WHO REMEMBER THE LIBERATION OF OUR ANCESTORS AS IF WE OURSELVES WERE THERE, WILL ACT TO LIBERATE OURSELVES!

What can we do? We can cut all our ties to the Empires of the Pharaohs. As individuals, and through groups such as churches and synagogues, we can withdraw our bank deposits and sell our stock holdings, and put our resources into cooperative ventures, nonprofit housing, and banks which finance inner city housing redevelopment. We can begin campaigns to selectively boycott oil companies which profit from pollution and imperialism. We must remember that we ourselves pollute the air and promote imperialism as long as we live inside a system that does so. Why not set aside a contribution to changing that system (through an anti-war or other movement group) each time you purchase gasoline? Collectively we have allowed the Pharaohs to enslave us . . . collectively is the only way we will achieve liberation.

OUT OF SLAVERY, FREEDOM.
ME-AVDUT L'CHERUT!

Sources: *Fortune Magazine, Dun and Bradstreet's Million Dollar Directory, Moody's Bank and Finance Manual, The Empire of High Finance* by Victor Perlo, *The Politics of Oil* by Robert Engler, *NACLA Newsletter,* North American Congress on Latin America, *The Newspaper,* of the Committee for a Democratic Society, of Rockefeller University, and *30¢ For What?: The New York City*

Transit Crisis by the Joint Committee on Transit, New York, New York, December 1969.

III—A Liturgy for Sukkot, to be Read after the Biblical "Seven Days" of Creation.
Written by Gary Schaer and Read by Jews for Urban Justice
Sukkot, 5731—October 14, 1970

And on His first day, Man defied the acts of God and performed his daily works. And lo, in His beginning Man took the light that had been created for Him and made it the same as night. And over the face of the earth, a great darkness was formed spreading from the heights of the mountains and extending to the depths of the valleys. And Man looked across His lands and saw His crops would not grow and His animals would not reproduce. And seeing that it was not for His good, Man made the constant darkness into constant light. And over the face of the earth, the sun shone and Man saw that it was for His good; for the crops grew and His animals bore others in their form. And the morning and the noon were the first of His days.

And Man said, Let Me make the oceans and the rivers small and upon them let the wastes of My body and the wastes of the creations I have made flow. And let them be for carriers of that which serves Me no need and let them be condensed so that My crops may grow more and My animals may bear others like themselves. And let my children and those that follow them live upon the newly formed lands. And Man called the lands from the oceans His and waters for His wastes did He call His also and He saw that it was good. And the morning and the noon were the second of His days.

And Man said, Let Me take the grasses of the earth

that serve Me no good and destroy them. Let them that does that which I covet multiply but that which does me no good shall I destroy. And with His creations of destruction did Man perform upon the grasses and the animals which fed upon the grasses acts which made them lifeless. And it was so. And the earth which housed them became barren of them and all which Man did not wish to be destroyed as well. And the creatures which Man had desired no longer visited the plains of their habitat. And lo, much of what Man had desired to be destroyed remained upon the earth. And the insects and the pestilence of the earth became fruitful and multiplied in the mountains of His waste. And Man saw that it was not good. And the morning and the noon were the third of His days.

And Man said, Let me form the seasons as I have formed the days and devoid them of darkness. And let the snow from the heavens and maladies be stopped and all the seasons be one. And it was so. And seeing the stars shine as one and the seasons as one, Man saw His work was good. And seeing the latter portion of His day less bright than His first, Man shot to the stars that once shone in the night a great force of His energy that made them rival the daylight. And the stars became lights during the day and lights during the latter day and all that remained was bright during the time of the day and the time when once there was darkness. And the division of the night from the day and the seasons from one another was ended and all became one. And Man saw that He had created and determined it for His good. And the morning and the morning that was once the noon was the fourth of His day.

And Man said, Let Me make one as Myself and destroy all those unlike Me. And Man created from His firmament the tools to make Himself and did he perform His wish. So from His instruments, Man did perform His desire to make His form reproduce. And seeing that those He had created needed more structures in which to dwell, Man made his seas still smaller and took the wastes that flowed upon them and did He place them in mountains. And the animals which had not been destroyed lived upon the wastes and became plentiful and Man could not control their bestiality. And the form of Man became fruitful and so did He multiply plentifully. And the food that he sought to feed His reproduced form burned from the rays of the constant light and His children became starved. And the morning and the morning that was once the noon was the fifth of His days.

And Man said, Behold My creations for they are not good. So Man took from His hands the instruments He had created and fashioned them as weapons of conflict. And upon the animals which visited upon the mountains of His wastes, Man placed foods of death to perish them from His earth. And lo, the animals which ate of the foods were destroyed as the others like them. And upon the land did there come a great and mighty famine and Man took his weapons so that He might kill others like Him for food for His children. And lo, the earth was barren of the plants and the animals which fed upon them and the stars in the days and the stars in the night grew hot. And the morning and the morning that was once the noon was the sixth of His days.

And Man viewed His creations on the seventh of His days and He saw that they were not good. And the morning of the morning of the seventh saw from the river depths a great cloud of smoke that rose in the form of the trees that were no more. And from the depths of the oceans and of the seas of the lands the smoke did rise unto the heavens. And lo, the morning and the morning that was once the noon was the seventh day. And all that remained, rested.

IV—Excerpts from the First Book of Maccabees,
Excerpts Read by Jews for Urban Justice
At a Chanukah Celebration in front of the
Soviet Embassy,
December 22, 1970

"At that time there appeared in Israel a group of renegade Jews, who incited the people. 'Let us enter into a covenant with the Gentiles round about,' they said, 'because disaster upon disaster has overtaken us since we segregated ourselves from them.' The people thought this a good argument, and some of them in their enthusiasm went to the king and received authority to introduce non-Jewish laws and customs. They built a sports-stadium in the gentile style in Jerusalem. They removed their marks of circumcision and repudiated the holy covenant. They intermarried with Gentiles, and abandoned themselves to evil ways.

"When he was firmly established on his throne, Antiochus made up his mind to become king of Egypt and so to rule over both kingdoms. He assembled a powerful force of chariots, elephants, and cavalry, and a great fleet, and invaded Egypt. When battle was joined, Ptolemy king of Egypt was seized with panic and took to flight, leaving many dead. The fortified towns were captured and the land pillaged.

"On his return from the conquest of Egypt, in the year 143, Antiochus marched with a strong force against Israel and Jerusalem. In his arrogance he entered the temple and carried off the golden altar, the lamp-stand with all its equipment, the table for the Bread of the Presence, the sacred cups and bowls, the golden censers, the curtain, and the crowns. He stripped off all the gold plating from the temple front. He seized the silver, gold, and precious vessels, and whatever secret treasures he found, and took them all with him when he left for his own country. He had caused much bloodshed, and he gloated over all he had done. . . .

"The king then issued a decree throughout his empire: his subjects were all to become one people and abandon their own laws and religion. The nations everywhere complied with the royal command, and many in Israel accepted the foreign worship, sacrificing to idols and profaning the sabbath. Moreover, the king sent agents with written orders to Jerusalem and the towns of Judaea. Ways and customs foreign to the country were to be introduced. Burnt-offerings, sacrifices, and libations in the temple were forbidden; sabbaths and feast-days were to be profaned; the temple and its ministers to be defiled. Altars, idols, and sacred precincts to be established; swine and other unclean beasts to be offered in sacrifice. They must leave their sons uncircumcised; they must make themselves in every way abominable, unclean, and profane, and so forget the law and change all their statutes. The penalty for disobedience was death.

"Such was the decree which the king issued to all his subjects. He appointed superintendents over all the people, and instructed the towns of Judaea to offer sacrifice, town by town. People thronged to their side in large numbers, every one of them a traitor to the law. Their wicked conduct throughout the land drove Israel into hiding in every possible place of refuge.

"On the fifteenth day of the month Kislev in the year 145, 'the abomination of desolation' was set up on the altar. Pagan altars were built throughout the towns of Judaea; incense was offered at the doors of houses and in the streets. All scrolls of the law which were found were torn up and burnt. Anyone discovered in possession of a Book of the Covenant, or conforming to the law, was put to death by the king's sentence. Thus month after month these wicked men used their power against the Israelites whom they found in their towns.

"On the twenty-fifth day of the month they offered sacrifice on the pagan altar which was on top of the altar of the Lord. In accordance with the royal decree, they put to death women who had had their children circumcised. Their babies, their families, and those who had circumcised them, they hanged by the neck. Yet many in Israel found strength to resist, taking a determined stand against eating any unclean food. They welcomed death rather than defile themselves and profane the holy covenant, and so they died. The divine wrath raged against Israel.

"At this time a certain Mattathias, son of John, son of Symeon, appeared on the scene. He was a priest of the Joarib family from Jerusalem, who had settled at Modin. Mattathias had five sons, John called Graddis, Simon called Thassis, Judas called Maccabaeus, Eleazar called Avaran, and Jonathan called Apphus.

"When Mattathias saw the sacrilegious acts committed in Judaea and Jerusalem, he said:

'Oh! Why was I born to see this,
the crushing of my people, the ruin of the holy city?
They sat idly by when it was surrendered,
when the holy place was given up to the alien.
Her temple is like a man robbed of honour;
its glorious vessels are carried off as spoil.
Her infants are slain in the street,
her young men by the sword of the foe.
Is there a nation that has not usurped her sovereignty,
a people that has not plundered her?
She has been stripped of all her adornment,
no longer free, but a slave.

Now that we have seen our temple with all its beauty and splendour laid waste and profaned by the Gentiles, why should we live any longer?' So Mattathias and his sons tore their garments, put on sackcloth, and mourned bitterly.

"The king's officers who were enforcing apostasy came to the town of Modin to see that sacrifice was offered, and many Israelites went over to them. Mattathias and his sons stood in a group. The king's officers spoke to Mattathias: 'You are a leader here,' they said, 'a man of mark and influence in this town, with your sons and brothers at your back. You be the first now to come forward and carry out the king's order. All the nations have done so, as well as the leading men in Judaea and the people left in Jerusalem. Then you and your sons will be enrolled among the King's Friends; you will all receive high honours, rich rewards of silver and gold, and many further benefits.'

"To this Mattathias replied in a ringing voice: 'Though all the nations within the king's dominions obey him and forsake their ancestral worship, though they have chosen to submit to his commands, yet I and my sons and brothers will follow the covenant of our fathers. Heaven forbid we should ever abandon the law and its statutes. We will not obey the command of the king, nor will we deviate one step from our forms of worship.'

"As soon as he had finished, a Jew stepped forward in full view of all to offer sacrifice on the pagan altar at Modin, in obedience to the royal command. The sight stirred Mattathias to indignation; he shook with passion, and in a fury of righteous anger rushed forward and slaughtered the traitor on the very altar. At the same time he killed the officer sent by the king to enforce sacrifice, and pulled the pagan altar down. Thus Mattathias showed his fervent zeal for the law, just as Phinehas had done by killing Zimri son of Salu. 'Follow me,' he shouted through the town, 'every one of you who is zealous for the law and strives to maintain the covenant.' He and his sons took to the hills, leaving all their belongings behind in the town.

"At that time many who wanted to maintain their religion and law went down to the wilds to live there. They took their sons, their wives, and their cattle with them, for their miseries were more than they could bear. Word soon reached the king's officers and the forces in Jerusalem, the city of David, that men who had defied the king's order had gone down into hiding-places in the wilds. A large body of men went quickly after them, came up with them, and occupied positions opposite. They prepared to attack them on the sabbath. 'There is still time,' they shouted; 'come out, obey the king's command, and your lives will be spared.' 'We will not come out,' the Jews replied; 'we will not obey the king's command or profane the sabbath.' Without more ado the attack was launched; but the Israelites did nothing in reply; they neither hurled stones, nor barricaded their caves. 'Let us all meet death with a clear conscience,' they said; 'we call heaven and earth to testify that there is no justice in this slaughter.' So they were attacked and massacred on the sabbath, men, women, and children, up to a thousand in all, and their cattle with them.

"Great was the grief of Mattathias and his friends when they heard the news. They said to one another, 'If we all do as our brothers have done, if we refuse to fight the Gentiles for our lives as well as for our laws and customs, then they will soon wipe us off the face of the earth.' That day they decided that, if anyone came to fight against them on the sabbath, they would fight back, rather than all die as their brothers in the caves had done.

"It was then that they were joined by a company of Hasidaeans, stalwarts of Israel, every one of them a volunteer in the cause of the law; and all who were refugees from the troubles came to swell their numbers, and so add to their strength. Now that they had an organized force, they turned their wrath on the guilty men and renegades. Those who escaped their fierce attacks took refuge with the Gentiles.

"Mattathias and his friends then swept through the country, pulling down the pagan altars, and forcibly circumcising all the uncircumcised boys found within the frontiers of Israel. They hunted down their arrogant enemies, and the cause prospered in their hands. Thus they saved the law from the Gentiles and their kings, and broke the power of the tyrant . . .

"Judas then appointed leaders of the people, officers over thousands, hundreds, fifties, and tens. As the law commands, he ordered back to their homes those who were building their houses or were newly wed or who were planting vineyards, or who were faint-hearted. Thereupon the army moved and took up their positions to the south of Emmaus, where Judas thus addressed them: 'Prepare for action and show yourselves men. Be ready at dawn to fight these Gentiles who are massed against us to destroy us and our holy place. Better die fighting than look on while calamity overwhelms our people and the holy place. But it will be as Heaven wills.' . . .

"Judas said to his men: 'Do not be afraid of their great numbers or panic when they charge. Remember how our fathers were saved at the Red Sea, when Pharaoh and his army were pursuing them. Let us cry now to Heaven to favour our cause, to remember the covenant made with our fathers, and to crush this army before us today. Then all the Gentiles will know that there is One who saves and liberates Israel.' . . .

"But Judas and his brothers said 'Now that our enemies have been crushed, let us go up to Jerusalem to cleanse the temple and rededicate it.' So the whole army was assembled and went up to Mount Zion. There they found the temple laid waste, the altar profaned, the gates burnt down, the courts overgrown like a thicket or wooded hillside, and the priests' rooms in ruin. They tore their garments, wailed loudly, put ashes on their heads, and fell on their faces to the ground. They sounded the ceremonial trumpets, and cried aloud to Heaven.

"Then Judas detailed troops to engage the garrison of the citadel while he cleansed the temple. He selected priests without blemish, devoted to the law, and they purified the temple, removing to an unclean place the stones which defiled it. They discussed what to do with the altar of burnt-offering, which was profaned, and rightly decided to demolish it, for fear it might become a standing reproach to them because it had been defiled by the Gentiles. They therefore pulled down the altar, and stored away the stones in a fitting place on the temple hill, until a prophet should arise who could be consulted about them. They took unhewn stones, as the law commands, and built a new altar on the model of the previous one. They rebuilt the temple and restored its interior, and consecrated the temple courts. They renewed the sacred vessels and the lamp-stand, and brought the altar of incense and the table into the temple. They burnt incense on the altar and lit the lamps on the lamp-stand to shine within the temple. When they had put the Bread of the Presence on the table and hung the curtains, all their work was completed.

"Then, early on the twenty-fifth day of the ninth month, the month Kislev, in the year 148, sacrifice was offered as the law commands on the newly made altar of burnt-offering. On the anniversary of the day when the Gentiles had profaned it, on that very day, it was rededicated, with hymns of thanksgiving, to the music of harps and lutes and cymbals. All the people prostrated themselves, worshipping and praising Heaven that their cause had prospered.

"They celebrated the rededication of the altar for eight days."

V—Inaction: A Diatribe
Written by Michael Tabor of JUJ for his
Weekly Column and Published by the
Jewish Post and Opinion
January 15, 1971

One question which elicits more reaction than anything else, concerns American Jewish inaction during the Holocaust. Only infrequently do middle-age Jews admit their relative apathy (once, after a heated four-hour discussion a group of people admitted they were more concerned and involved in "making-it" in America than in risking their position here for the sake of their European brethren)—usually I get the "good German" we-didn't-know-it-was-happening reaction.

Reading *While 6 Million Died* by Arthur D. Morse (Ace Books, 1967, 75 cents) confirmed some of my assumptions. American institutional Jewish leadership (with the possible exception of the American Jewish Congress, the Jewish Labor BUND and a number of Jewish socialist-labor-Marxist groups) decided that the best course was one of quiet, behind-the-scenes, negotiation, pressure, and prodding. The American Jewish Committee and B'nai B'rith should never have been allowed to resume their pre-war prominence after their disgraceful and costly performance during the Holocaust. The American Jewish establishment wasted precious months of time by applying polite and gentle persuasion tactics on the State Department and F.D.R. while from 1933 on they knew many of the brutalities of the Nazis.

NAHUM GOLDMANN ONCE RECALLED the time a cable came from the Warsaw Ghetto to Rabbi Stephen Wise asking why Jewish leaders in the U.S. had not held a day and night vigil in front of the White House demading that the President bomb the extermination camps. Yuri Suhl, in *They Fought Back* (Paperback Library, 1968, P. 134, 75 cents) reports that Goldmann later lamented ". . . we did not go beyond routine petitions and requests, and because the Jewish communities did not have the courage and the daring to exert pressure on the democratic government by drastic means and to force them to take drastic measures."

Indeed, the heroes of the Holocaust are all but forgotten. How many children in most American Jewish "religious schools" would recognize the names Szmul Zygielbojm, Mordechai Anielevich, Yitzchok Zuckerman, Bernard Goldstein or even Emmanuel Ringelblum?

Anyway, who am I to talk? I did not really live through the era. I did not have to face the tragic options open to American Jewry. Perhaps my only actions would have involved attending a Madison Square Garden Rally, or a Protest March or sending money. But the reaction of American Jewry to the Leningrad Trials brought it all back home.

Exactly what did American Jewry do? In Washington, D.C. 250 "leaders" met, condemned, praised, lauded, and lobbied. Later, when it was time for more direct action, they attempted to march to the Soviet Embassy (from which they quickly scurried away when threatened with arrest). Thirteen Washington-area rabbis, supposedly worried because it only seemed as if students were getting arrested in past demonstrations at the Embassy decided to take the big step and spend eleven minutes directly in front of the Embassy. When the cops came, one rabbi "fearlessly" stalled them with questions until the group finished praying, at which point they all hustled off.

(How would it have looked if a group of eleven rabbis announced that they would vigil at the Embassy one-by-one and face possible arrest, until the eleven prisoners were released? Oi, what embarrassment!) The Jewish Community Council of Greater Washington sponsored a "mass protest" rally, which I attended. It consisted of a bunch of rhetorical speeches, some singing and a candle-light march to the White House and then more speeches. They carefully avoided going closer to the Soviet Embassy than the five hundred feet the law allowed (ironically enacted in the early 1930s to keep Jews a safe distance from the German Embassy.) The low point of this "protest" came when the President of the Council said, "The U.S. has a glorious record of having interceded in the past on behalf of oppressed groups in other lands." (Was he jokingly referring to Vietnam, Cambodia, or sarcastically to Jews in Nazi concentration camps? Perhaps he was referring to the massive emergency relief program of four helicopters Nixon sent to Pakistan when hundreds of thousands of people were perishing and begged for help????)

Out of the 100,000-plus Jewish population of Washington, something like two thousand turned out for the pathetic rally. In New York City, unless I misunderstood the newspaper reports, three thousand people turned out for the main protest. Where was everyone else? Cursing the Soviet Union during the supper TV reports? Burping their indignation? Did they think that their own presence at the rally was meaningless? Did attendance mean losing time from work? Or were some of them wary of becoming part of a protest that made it seem as if the Soviet government was the only oppressor, and thus becoming part of the anti-Communist cold war strategy?

In Washington, D.C., some of us were concerned about this problem and attempted to broaden our protest to include opposition to all forms of oppression. Being concerned about anti-Semitism in Russia, rather than racism in all its forms narrows (perhaps even excludes) other forms of bigotry against other people. Unfortunately, thirteen of us were arrested in front of the Soviet Embassy before we were able to start a special, last evening of Chanukah.

MANY NON-JEWS AND JEWS in much more precarious positions reacted a bit more forcefully. In Genoa,

Italy, thousands of longshoremen refused to unload Russian and Spanish ships. In Russia, where Jewish dissent almost automatically means imprisonment, a dozen sympathizers of the defendants stood outside the Supreme Court building for three days in the rain and snow until the sentences were commuted. And when a high-ranking Soviet cop ordered a protester to remove his symbolic yellow Star of David, the man refused.

All right, it's over now. The brief show of indignation can stop. And now brothers Kuznetsov and Dymshits will die their "slow death" in the work camps. So "Jewish leadership" may now go back and resume their awesome tasks of dedicating our beautifully new multi-million dollar community centers and synagogues, attending those wonderfully exciting Miami Beach conventions and conferences, raising money for Israel and against defamation and generally, pursuing the task we're apparently very able to perform—"making-it" in Amerika.

*From the Burning Bush
to Sinai*

V

From the Burning Bush to Sinai

One way in which the tradition talks about the moment that we seek is as the "Passover of the Messianic Age," modeled on but growing beyond our "Passover of the Generations." In that great day the Jewish imagination saw the liberation of all the peoples from political and spiritual slavery, in order that all might gather at a new Sinai. We might therefore try to understand what such a crisis would be like by looking more closely at the model: at the Exodus which liberated the Jewish People. And if we try to understand the Exodus as a model, our attention is drawn at once to the teaching that the Exodus itself was modeled upon a smaller, lesser model. Its leader Moses played out first in his own life a model of what the People then played out in theirs. He moved from an individual rebellion and flight—his own exodus—through exile and meditation to the moment of his own "private" Sinai at the Burning Bush. It was this prefiguring that made him a prophet, this living through a political and spiritual liberation in his own life that made him a fit leader for the liberation of the People. And the growth from individual to communal liberation turns upon the moment of the Burning Bush, when Moses recognizes the command to free his people.

What happened to him at the Burning Bush is therefore crucial. He faces there a God Who asserts simultaneously that One is old and new: the God of Abraham, the God of Isaac, the God of Jacob—that is, the ancient God of the People of Israel—but a God who now is to be known by a name that Abraham, Isaac, and Jacob had not been allowed to know One by: "I Am Becoming What I Am Becoming."

Let us leave aside for a moment that question which some theists and some atheists are obsessed by: was this God "real" or did Moses invent One? We can come back to the question. But to Moses, and then to the People, the God felt real enough. So for us, what is important in order to understand the Exodus is that first Moses, and then the Jewish People, had to face an agony of growth. The agony felt real enough to them. They could not simply follow the dictates of an old and familiar God, the God called "The Almighty" that Abraham, Isaac, and Jacob knew and more or less understood. But they could not abandon that God either, for a new one. The old God was not dead; but One had metamorphosed. Indeed, One had defined Oneself as the God of Metamorphosis: "I Am Becoming What I Am Becoming."

Why? Why was not the God of the fathers enough?

Because the bitterness of slavery was so great that the God of Jacob, who countenanced that slavery, seemed inadequate to the task of liberation?

Let us take a deep breath before we remove the question mark from that answer. For if that is indeed the answer, we may stand today at the Burning Bush—again.

For to our whole People, the Holocaust is surely what the nightmare of one enslaved kinsman was to Moses. To all the world, Hiroshima and the Holocaust are surely what the nightmare of slavery in Egypt was to the whole Jewish People.

We, the Jewish People, are Moses at the Burning Bush.

We are Moses, facing a God who has not been adequate, under One's old names and knowledges, to prevent the destruction of all humanity.

And what is it that burns and burns, yet is not consumed?

We ourselves. The smoke that rose at Auschwitz and Hiroshima was our smoke: but we are not consumed. Yet.

If we hear the Voice, we shall not be consumed; if we do not hear, we shall.

We are both Moses and the Bush. Our own suffering is our own revelation.

We must discover the new Name of One who is holy, in order to liberate ourselves and all the world, in order to create the Passover of All the Nations, in order to make the trek to Sinai.

We, the Jewish People, have responded to the Holocaust as Moses first responded to the beating of his kinsman, his own rebellious slaying of the taskmaster, and his fear of discovery: with a flight from the Pharaohs of the modern super-states, with a turmoil of spirit, a troubled meditation in the hills of Midian, an interim sojourn among the flocks on a rocky land outside the modern Egypts.

That sojourn was necessary for us, as it was for Moses. But it is not enough. We must return into Egypt, speak the new Name of God, and join with the other peoples to liberate us all.

Why us? We are slow and stammering of action, as Moses was slow and stammering of speech. Our children are not circumcised of thought and action, as his son was not circumcised of body. Why us?

He went because the command came from out of the Burning Bush; he went because the command came from what he believed was the God of Abraham, Isaac, and Jacob—though newly named; he went because the alternative was despair or death for himself and death or despair for his people. He went, at last, because he did not need to go alone: he was promised the help of Aaron, he achieved the help of Miriam, he was given the help of Egyptians in that "mixed multitude" which departed from Egypt.

And us?

Must we go alone, lead alone, liberate alone? No; there will be many Aarons, many Miriams, many "Egyptians"

—a mixed multitude. Our brother and sister peoples càn rise with us.

Must we go at all? There is nothing but despair and death for us if we do not act. We could refuse, but by refusing we reject our whole history and deny our whole selves. By refusing we would betray, if not the God of Abraham, Isaac, and Jacob, then Abraham, Isaac, and Jacob themselves; if not the God of Moses, Micah, and Isaiah, then Moses, Micah, and Isaiah themselves. We would betray the whole thirty-five hundred years of both the Vision and the Path: the vision of the Messianic Age, the path of a halachic community. For in this sense, let us be clear, it is not important to know whether the God of Abraham and the God of Isaiah "really and truly" created Heaven and Earth and divided the Red Sea; it is enough to know that the Jewish People was formed around that belief, created Judaism out of that belief, shaped even such "nonreligious" ideas as political Zionism and Bundism out of the deposit left by that belief, and can hardly refuse to deal with the supreme crisis in its own and the world's history, a crisis foreseen by that belief . . . can hardly refuse that obligation without ceasing to be Jewish.

There is no obligation to accept the obligation easily or joyfully. Moses argued with the Voice from the Burning Bush; indeed, the tradition is clear that the God of Abraham, Jacob, and Moses is precisely the God with which one strives and struggles. That our People will strive against acceptance of the burden must not only be expected, but perhaps celebrated—how else could we be sure that the burden belongs to us? Moses validated his leadership by being realistic about his failings: "My voice falters, the people will not believe me; choose someone else." If we blithely rush to the barricades, we don't belong there. But let us not turn a deaf ear to the Voice; let us take our history seriously enough to engage in a struggle, a debate. It will be even harder because as the tradition says, no one among us will be a prophet like

Moses—and indeed, no one among us will be a prophet at all. It is we, collectively, the Jewish People, who stand before the Bush and collectively ask ourselves and That Other whether the burden is ours to lift.

Is the Other truly there?

I believe One is there. I do not believe in an orthodox way, I do not even believe as Buber does. But I do feel myself attracted by a reversal of the profession of belief that Buber makes: "Man, while created by God, was established by Him in an independence which has since remained undiminished. In this independence he stands over against God. . . . Man can say Thou to Him, stand face to face with Him, have intercourse with Him. . . . So man takes part with full freedom and spontaneity in the dialogue between the two which forms the essence of existence."

Let us see what happens if we try to reverse that profession of belief. Let us try to say that it was not God who broke through to Abraham, but Abraham who broke through to imagine a God that was not an idol. Let us try to say that it was not God who handed down the Torah, but Moses who wrestled mightily to bring his people the Torah down from Sinai. Very well: does that mean we can ignore the results, the collective judgment, the Spirit of the People, that they called God?

No, it does not. It is a false, a silly, a superficial rationalism that proclaims that if human beings created God instead of discovering him, then God must not exist. I feel attracted to profess: *God, while created by Humanity was established by us in an independence which has since remained undiminished.* . . . So God stands over against us, says Thou to us, takes part with full freedom in the dialogue with us which forms the essence of our existence. . . . An independence that is undiminished, but not unchanged: for if Humanity must say Thou to God, hear Thou from God, stand face to face with God, then surely the Wrestle of the two changes them both. Moses was changed by the Burning Bush; but the challenge that

Moses, out of his memory of despair and death in Egypt, directed to the Bush—What Shall I Tell Them Is Your Name?—changed the Name of God, forced God to respond as One responded to Abraham's challenge before Sodom.

If it was Humanity that created God, how is that God different from the idols? Why bother to address One at all, why not abandon One—as those have done who have responded to the Holocaust, or Hiroshima, by proclaiming the death of God and the emptiness of their own lives? I do not necessarily mean those who have used the specific phrase, "death of God": some of them have not meant God's disappearance from their lives, but a reappearance without dogma. But some Jews have felt that after Auschwitz, nothing remained of the great mission except bare physical survival. But even if we see this as part of the retreat into Midian, to be treated with love and understanding, it is too easy for this outlook to erect the Jewish People itself into an idol. What distinguishes the idols from God, if Humanity creates both God and idols?

The Psalmist tells us what idols are: They have eyes and see not, mouths and taste not, hands and feel not. . . . They are dead, and those who make them become like them. God, on the other hand, is alive; Humanity is made in the image of God, or God in the image of Humanity: alive, changing, unpredictable. The human beings who create God continue to live; the human beings who make idols die.

That is the difference, and that is the touchstone by which we know the difference. Let us be clear: the difference is immense, and urgent for us. Because the Holocaust and Hiroshima can only mean one of two things: either God is indeed dead, or so alive, so full of life, that a great Metamorphosis is imminent. That the same old God can survive the Holocaust and Hiroshima is inconceivable. If God is truly dead, then it was always an idol —and we who made it are about to die. But if it is truly

God Whom we created, then we are both alive; and precisely because God is alive, One can grow and change for us as One did for Moses—so that we and the world can live, as Moses and his people did.

If we created the God of Abraham and the God of Moses, then the responsibility for the inadequacy of that God rests upon us. As Moses challenged the Bush, so we must challenge. But the new Name must issue from the Other. That is the implication of saying that it is a new Name, not a new God, we search for; it is from the God of Abraham and the God of Moses that we must hear the Voice. It is out of our tradition that the Voice will speak to us; not *caught within*, but *growing from* our tradition, developing that of the tradition which is hesitant, faltering—but at this moment necessary. That is the meaning of saying that we are speakers in a Conversation, not shouting braggarts in an echo chamber; that we truly created a living God rather than inventing an idol.

Our task, like that of Moses, is to challenge—and to hear. To hear the Name.

What is it? What Name comes forth from the Bush—from our own suffering, our own striving?

I don't know. If it is now the whole People that is the prophet, only the whole People can fully hear the Voice. Till then, each of us can only barely feel a trembling, a shaking in the air before the Voice speaks from the Bush. Some of us, straining, may feel that shaking as a wisp of inclination: If the Name of the God of Abraham was Power, All-mightiness, the thrust of a Thesis; if the Name of the God of Moses was not the Antithesis but the Thesis-Antithesis, the Becoming, the Dialectic; then the name of the God of our People in our generation might be the Synthesis, the Harmonizing, the End of Alienation, *Shalom*.

And that, of course, would accord with the Messianic vision: the end of the alienation of nation from nation, of men from women, of men and women from their work, of body from mind and action from ideas, of human beings from nature, of God from the Shechinah, the very Presence of God.

The Bush is burning, but the Voice has not yet spoken aloud; we can only feel, guess, hope: we cannot yet hear. But it may be that we must act even before we hear: *Naaseh v' nishma;* that we must act *in order* to hear.

Let us then act.

Let us then create.

Let us then begin to live as we would imagine the Voice might ask us. To achieve such parts of the new Halacha as we feel might accord with a God named *Shalom.*

Those of us who recognize that the Bush is aflame again must come together to write and live that new Halacha. I can only suggest some of the issues that, it seems to me, we will have to face:

To reexamine the relations between the sexes in Judaism from the very bottom. The God of Abraham, Isaac, and Jacob was specifically never called the God of Sarah, Rebecca, Rachel, and Leah; the prophecies of Miriam and Deborah never became central texts like those of Moses and Isaiah. The gifts of women have never been called to the central celebrations and studies of the Path and the gifts of men have never been fully called to its walking. There are hints in the Torah, the Talmud, and the legends of a deep fear and suspicion of both women and the Motherness of God. The femaleness of the Shechina has been in exile these many centuries. Yes, there are also hints that the Holy One is both male and female—but the hints must be made clear, the fusion must be achieved and fully understood by us. For it may well be that the inadequacy of God under One's old Names to prevent the rape of the world environment, the Holocaust and Hiroshima, was connected with that very exile of femaleness. If the God that we created was imbued, in the realm of sexuality as in other realms, with some of our defects as well as with our best hopes, then let us strive in facing the Bush to create among ourselves a new Halacha of sexuality. For if in our new Halacha we reconstruct the relations between men and women, then it might become true that in the Other's new Name the fusion of male and female could be more fully achieved and understood than in the Names we have known One by in the past.

To reexamine the meaning of Kashrut. There can be no doubt that in a halachic society, food as well as other elements of daily physical life must come under the review of concepts of holiness, justice, freedom, equality. The old specific code is more in question. Ought food drenched in chemicals, food wrenched from the soil and sea through violence to the World, food grown in any but communal or democratic-collective farms or sold through any but cooperative stores, be considered Kosher? Ought the new Kashrut be vegetarian?

To reexamine the intention—and the practice—of the Sabbatical and Jubilee years. In our days, the exclusion of property in cities from the periodic total redistribution of property could not meet the needs of a new halachic community; and indeed the Halacha of *Shalom* may simply require the equal sharing, not the periodic redistribution, of all wealth.

To reexamine the institutions of War and the State. Surely the new Halacha would link itself to Samuel's vision of the people without a king as well as to Isaiah's vision of the peoples without war. The abolition of War and the State means taking the Path of decentralized, self-governing communities of human beings at work and celebration: federated, but not bureaucratized. The Path of more fully liberated kibbutzim.

To reexamine our great Holy Days. The new Halacha must express in joy and sadness the links of the Jewish People to the other peoples. We might, for example, develop Tisha B'Av as a memorial not only of the Temple in Jerusalem but also of the Holocaust and Hiroshima—those modern warnings of the Destruction of the Temple of Mankind. In this and similar ways we could join in the universal experiences of Humanity without abandoning our own selves.

There are some who would say—critically, angrily—that what I have described is a new religion, not Judaism at all. There are others—among them two rabbis, Martin Siegel and Everett Gendler—who have begun to speak of a new religious community that cuts across the old boundaries between Judaism and Christianity, and perhaps even between them and other Paths as well. Certainly many of us working in the radical Jewish movement feel an affinity with such "underground" Christians as the Berrigans, and they with us—more than we can feel with Jews who serve as chief clerks for the Empire in its wasting of Indochina, more than they can feel for the Cardinals who bless the bombs. Perhaps all those who oppose idolatry will in this great Crisis of the Idols find themselves learning far more deeply than they have ever learned before from Judaism and its ancient—though ever backsliding—struggle against idolatry. And on the other hand, Judaism once drank deeply of Aristotle, and not only survived but was reawakened to new life in the writings of the Rambam; Judaism today may learn from Marxism, Anarchism, Buddhism, Existentialism, and perhaps even from a reawakened Christianity of catacombs. Perhaps, then, our Paths are already crossing and even for occasional moments merging because we are struggling as never before for our lives and the life of The Other, against The Idols.

Perhaps there are other reasons, too, for thinking that some basic transformations of the religious sensibility lie just ahead. It would be surprising if the world transformation that is being worked by scientific "post-industrial" society were not to have some major effects on religious forms and approaches. Such "universal events" as Hiroshima and the Holocaust are almost bound to enter not only the narrowly political, but also the deeply religious realm of human thought and practice—across all the old boundaries. It may be that the "new class" which characteristically emerges in post-industrial society has a new kind of material relation to the means of production—a much more "idealist" relation that is based on holding information and knowledge. Does that not spur us to imagine a new consciousness of such a class, a consciousness that in essence is religious? The new class spans all the divisions of the developed countries into various "Easts" and "Wests"; does that portend a new transnational religious movement of great energy? Herbert Marcuse has written of the need for and the likelihood of a radical revaluation of values—"art," "sanity," "obscenity"—alongside changes in the distribution of wealth and power—indeed more important than such changes. He does not call such categories "religious," but they are.

We should not pretend to know where we will end up. It may be that we can achieve a community of linked and loving Paths that do not require us to be rigid about a "new" religion, or about the "old" ones. But I can only speak of what I feel; and that is that the historical experience transmitted to me, the symbols and celebrations that resonate in me, are somewhat different from those that speak best to my sisters and brothers who do not choose to be Jewish. It feels clear to me that my joy in being Jewish will remain, and that one part of what we build will be clearly Jewish. There was an "Old-New-Schul" in Prague; we can create a "New-Old-Judaism."

To imagine a new Halacha is to imagine a new Sinai. Somewhere on the long road from the Burning Bush to Sinai is where we stand—early in the road, since not even the new Name of God is yet available to us. That road for Moses was one of upheaval, agony, regret, as well as joy and triumph; and the rising of the whole world-wide Jewish People to the role of prophecy will be still harder. What is more, to create a brotherly-sisterly comradeship with other Peoples—Blacks, Vietnamese, Czechs, Palestinians, Chileans, Appalachians—will entail even more conflicts and jealousies than there were in the comradeship of Miriam, Aaron, and Moses, even more than in the mixed multitude that set out from Egypt. And our Pharaohs are more powerful, more dangerous, than those who ruled in Egypt.

The day is short, the task is enormous, the workers are exhausted; but the reward is great, and our Comrade is insistent. Many of us may not live to complete the task, all of us are free to evade it. But shall we?

Like Moses to Jethro: Let us return to our kinfolk in Egypt and see whether they be yet alive.

Going and Studying

Going and Studying

The sources for a radical Judaism are many and varied. They start with the Bible and continue in the Midrashic and Talmudic commentaries and in later rabbis and scholars. We can only hint at the depth and richness of the possibilities.

The most recent interpretation of the Bible as theologically and politically radical is Erich Fromm's *You Shall Be as Gods*. But see also Martin Buber's *Moses, I and Thou, Good and Evil*, and his works on Chasidism; and Abraham J. Heschel, *The Prophets*, and *The Sabbath*.

For the various fusions of Marxist, Anarchist, and Jewish thought, see Ezra Mendelsohn, *Class Struggle in the Pale*, on the origins of the Jewish Labor Bund; Ber Borochov's various writings on Socialist Zionism (for example, in Arthur Hertzberg's *The Zionist Idea*); on Jewish-flavored communitarian anarchism and the kibbutz, Martin Buber, *Paths in Utopia*; and Isaac Deutscher, *The Non-Jewish Jew*.

On the question of the Diaspora, see the work of Simon Dubnow and Simon Rawidowicz.

For more recent radical Jewish writing, see the scattered writings of Everett Gendler; Paul Jacobs, *Is Curly Jewish?* and *Between the Rock and the Hard Place*; Arthur I. Waskow, *The Freedom Seder: A New Haggadah for Passover*; Dan Leon, *The Kibbutz*; Michael Selzer, *The Wineskin and the Wizard*; Georges Friedmann, *The End of the Jewish People?*; Uri Avnery, *Israel Without Zionists*; Mike Tabor's column in the *Jewish Post and Opinion*; and (forthcoming) Bruce Goldman, *Up Against the Wailing Wall*.

Among newspapers and magazines carrying a range of radical Jewish thought are *The Voice of Micah*, 1808

Wyoming Ave., N.W., Washington, D.C.; *Response*, 415
South Street, Waltham, Mass.; *Jewish Urban Guerrilla*,
P.O. 19162, Washington, D.C.; *Brooklyn Bridge* c/o
Lubell & Lubell, 103 Park Avenue, New York, N.Y.;
The Jewish Review of Literature, 306 East 96 Street,
New York, N.Y.; *The Other Way*, 25 East 78 Street, New
York, N.Y.; and *Jewish Currents*, Room 601, 22 East 17
Street, New York, N.Y.

Two recent radical-Jewish films are available: one by
Bernard Timberg (2215 Ellsworth Street, Berkeley,
Calif.) on the Jewish radical movement in California,
and, from The Community of Micah, 1808 Wyoming
Ave., N.W. Washington, D.C., a film of the 1969 Free-
dom Seder in Washington, D.C. (Paperback copies of
The Freedom Seder are also available there.) There are
numerous recordings of Yiddish and Hebrew folk songs
and prayers, many of them radical. See especially Ruth
Rubin and Shlomo Carlebach.

The injunction to "go and study" is not only a matter
of books, films, and records. There are some people to
whom I owe special thanks for having directly argued
over these ideas with me. Not one of them fully agrees
with me; but all of them taught me a great deal, and I am
sure would be equally important to anyone who can
arrange to "study" with them: Robert Agus, Clement
Alexandre, Jeremy Brecher, Balfour Brickner, Shlomo
Carlebach, Uri Davis, Ivanhoe Donaldson, Gabrielle
Edgcomb, Bernard Fischmann, Simha Flapan, Marc Gell-
man, Everett Gendler, Mary Gendler, Todd Gitlin, Harold Goldberg, Bob Goldburg, Bruce Goldman, Paul
Goodman, Arthur Green, Bob Greenblatt, A. J. Heschel,
Paul Jacobs, Donald Jewell, Gerd Korman, Michael Ler-
ner, Dan Leon, Michael Maccoby, Bill Novak, Elye
Palevsky, Shirley Pallevsky, Susan Pasternack, Barbara
Raskin, Erika Raskin, Jamin Raskin, Marc Raskin, Leon-
ard Rodberg, Sharon Rose, John Ruskay, Josef Scharf-
Wilner, Emanuel Scherer, Marilyn Schlachter, Fran
Schreiberg, Steven Schwarzschild, David Shneyer, Chana

Siegel, Danny Siegel, Alan Solomonow, Arnold Sternberg, I. F. Stone, Mike Tabor, David Waskow, Irene Waskow, Shoshanna Waskow, Burt Weiss, Peter Weiss, Harold White, Mariette Wickes, Arnold Jacob Wolf, Jonathan Woocher, and Aviva Zuckoff.